Praise for *Two Trees Make a Forest*

A *New Statesman* Book of the Year

"*Two Trees Make a Forest* is a finely faceted meditation on memory, love, landscape—and finding a home in language. Its short, shining sections tilt yearningly toward one another; in form as well as content, this is a beautiful book about the distance between people and between places, and the means of their bridging." —ROBERT MACFARLANE, author of *Underland*

"Jessica J. Lee shows in this book how a delicate interrogation of language and place can be critical to understanding where we are going." —BONNIE TSUI, author of *Why We Swim*

"A subtle, powerful exploration of the relationship between people and place, and a luminous evocation of an extraordinary landscape." —MELISSA HARRISON, author of *All Among the Barley*

"Both clear-eyed and tenderhearted, *Two Trees Make a Forest* is a profound and gorgeously written meditation on the natural and familial environments that

shape us. Jessica J. Lee is a poetic talent keenly attentive to the mysterious and sublime."

—SHARLENE TEO, author of *Ponti*

"*Two Trees Make a Forest* takes a twisting path through mountain passes, over tree roots, by spoon-billed birds, and into a family's past. In this thoughtful memoir, Lee asks the reader to wonder, What makes a homeland? Is it language, family, landscape? I was left with a full heart and a longing to learn the name of each tree that lines my own past." —ROWAN HISAYO BUCHANAN, author of *Starling Days*

"There is so much loss in this family story—and in many family stories—and Lee has portrayed it with detail and restraint. Lee describes the complexities and anxieties of identity and language in a way that I know will have resonance with many readers, especially those with scattered families, disparate backgrounds. A beautiful, fully realized tribute to a family, and a brave, diligent search for understanding in the mist." —AMY LIPTROT, author of *The Outrun*

"*Two Trees Make a Forest* is a stunning book. It is full of family, longing, ghosts, and landscapes, all of which, in Lee's deft and beautiful telling, invoke the complications of belonging to worlds both human and natural. Lee's writing is alive equally to the details of forests and to the daily lives of her parents and grand-parents. The narrative emerges out of Taiwan's mists layer by layer, reminding us how place, experience, memory, and the bones of the earth remake one over time. A powerful meditation on the forces that shape our lives, from bedrock to the language we use to describe it." —BATHSHEBA DEMUTH, author of *Floating Coast*

Praise for *Turning*

National Post (Canada),
1 of the 99 Best Books of the Year

One of *Die Zeit*'s Best Books of the Year

A Notable Selection of the Sigurd F. Olson
Nature Writing Awards

Long-listed for the Frank Hegyi Award for
Emerging Authors

"A sublime, philosophical slipping into the deep. Her book, *Turning*, is filled with a wonderful melancholy as she swims through lakes laden with dark histories." —PHILIP HOARE, *New Statesman*

"A brilliant debut . . . There is clarity and pleasure in the swim's afterglow." —HARRIET BAKER, *The Times Literary Supplement*

"*Turning* is many things: a snapshot of Berlin seen through the prism of its lakes; the story of a broken and healing heart; a contemplation of identity; a coming-of-age story." —KATHARINE NORBURY, *The Observer*

"Bold and brave, she approaches her watery pilgrimage with a minimum amount of fuss. She doesn't, for instance, allow the ice on Brandenburg's lakes to get in her way, but takes a hammer to it . . . Lee writes like a siren, her silken prose blending with softly worn scholarship to enchanting effect. I challenge anyone to write more compellingly about Slavic suffixes or the formation of ice."

—OLIVER BALCH, *Literary Review*

"A lovely, poetic, sensuous and melancholy book." —JOSEPHINE FENTON, *Irish Examiner*

"The redemptive power of these wild landscapes, the changes in the water, and in Jessica, combine to create an inspiring story."   —*The Daily Telegraph*

"Jessica J. Lee's first book is lyrical and profound, told . . . in stunning prose and with poetic flare; it's poignant and moving and passionate . . . A lexeme masterpiece . . . Wafting sweetly even through the weighty bits, her musings as steady and tender in sadness as learned peace. Too intimate to be comfortable, but told with a piercing vulnerability so affecting you wind up feeling close to Lee anyway, side-by-side and stroke-by-stroke, solidarity in life and lake and existential slog, 52 times over, together better for it."
—TERRA ARNONE, *National Post* (Canada)

"Lee is an elegant writer; precise in her description, thoughtful in her observation, and most of all interested in the world that surrounds her . . . Jessica J. Lee's is a trip to the lake well worth taking, inspiring even this reluctant swimmer to reach for his swimming shorts."   —PAUL SCRATON, *Elsewhere*

"[Lee's] beautifully written memoir combines personal memories with geographic and historical observations that should resonate even for staunch landlubbers."
—*Metro*

"I loved this beautiful book. It's an attentive meditation on the pleasures and lessons of swimming in lakes, particularly in winter. Jessica J. Lee wears her bravery lightly and shares her knowledge with generosity. I recommend for outdoor swimmers or those who would like to be." —AMY LIPTROT, author of *The Outrun*

"Jessica J. Lee is a writer of rare and exhilarating grace. In *Turning*, she sounds the depths of lakes and her own life, never flinching from darkness, surfacing to fresh understandings of her place in the welter of natural and human history. A beautiful, moody, bracing debut." —KATE HARRIS, author of *Lands of Lost Borders*

"A deeply moving meditation on solitude, yearning, loss, and love. This lake of a book submerged and enveloped me. It is a truly beautiful offering." —KYO MACLEAR, author of *Birds Art Life*

"Lee's language is sharp as ice on a frozen lake. It's astounding how, to explore her past and her own shifting identity, she uses the land as a metaphor but tempers it with a view of yearning, the sight of someone once removed who can never really go back home again.

Insightful, unconventional, moving, and inspiring, I think this book will appeal to anyone who has ever struggled across the darkness trying to find the light."

—YASUKO THANH, author of
Mysterious Fragrance of the Yellow Mountains

TWO TREES
MAKE A FOREST

ALSO BY JESSICA J. LEE

Turning: A Year in the Water

TWO TREES
MAKE A FOREST

IN SEARCH OF
MY FAMILY'S PAST
AMONG TAIWAN'S
MOUNTAINS AND COASTS

JESSICA J. LEE

HAMISH HAMILTON
an imprint of Penguin Canada, a division of
Penguin Random House Canada Limited

Canada • USA • UK • Ireland • Australia • New Zealand •
India • South Africa • China

First published in Great Britain in 2019 by Virago Press,
an imprint of Little Brown Group
Published in Hamish Hamilton paperback by Penguin Canada, 2020
Simultaneously published in the United States by Catapult Books

www.penguinrandomhouse.ca

Epigraph from "The Papaya Tree" © 2017 by Brandon Shimoda
reprinted with permission of the author.

Excerpt from *Taiwan's Imagined Geography: Chinese Colonial
Travel Writing and Pictures, 1683–1895* by Emma Jinhua Teng.
Copyright © 2004 by the President and Fellows of Harvard College.
Reprinted with permission of the Harvard University Asia Center.

Excerpt from *Mountains of the Mind* © 2003 by Robert Macfarlane.
Reproduced with permission of Granta Books.

Excerpts from Liu Ka-shiang's "Small Is Beautiful" from *The Isle Full
of Noises,* edited by Dominic Cheung. Copyright © 1987 by Columbia
University Press. Reprinted with permission of the publisher.

Excerpt from Liu Ka-shiang's "Black-faced Spoonbill," *Interdisciplinary
Studies in Literature and Environment*, 2004, vol. 11, issue 2, pp. 268–69,
by permission of the Association for Literature and Environment.

Library and Archives Canada Cataloguing in Publication Data
is available upon request.
ISBN 9780735239579 (softcover) | ISBN 9780735239586 (ebook)

Cover illustration © Harriet Lee Merrion
Book design by Wah-Ming Chang
Calligraphy by Shih-Ming Chang

Printed and bound in the USA

10 9 8 7 6 5 4 3

For my family

Suddenly the tree was like the stake at the base of which the ashes of ghosts had cooled.

BRANDON SHIMODA
"The Papaya Tree"

A NOTE ON THE TEXT

LANGUAGE BARRIERS PLAY A PROMINENT ROLE in this story. Attentive readers of Chinese will note that, while I have used traditional Chinese characters, as is common in Taiwan, I've used a combination of the older Wade-Giles romanization system and Hanyu Pinyin (mainland Chinese) to transliterate names, places, and other details from Mandarin.

I've retained both forms in this book because usage in Taiwan and among those around me fluctuates—itself a lively illustration of the complexity of language in Taiwan today. Generally speaking, if I am writing about mainland China I have used Hanyu Pinyin, while for Taiwanese place-names I have mostly used Wade-Giles or occasionally the Tongyong Pinyin transliterations commonly used by local people and on signage. Google Maps—which uses Hanyu

Pinyin—renders the process of moving between digital maps and local usage somewhat complicated, so for places where Hanyu Pinyin has supplanted Wade-Giles (for example, Nenggao Mountain), I have used those names. For simplicity of reading between the two styles, I have omitted tone marks from my transliterations.

It should be noted that Wade-Giles is the preferred style of my elders; Hanyu Pinyin is what I was subsequently taught.

The gaps that bind us span more than the distances between words.

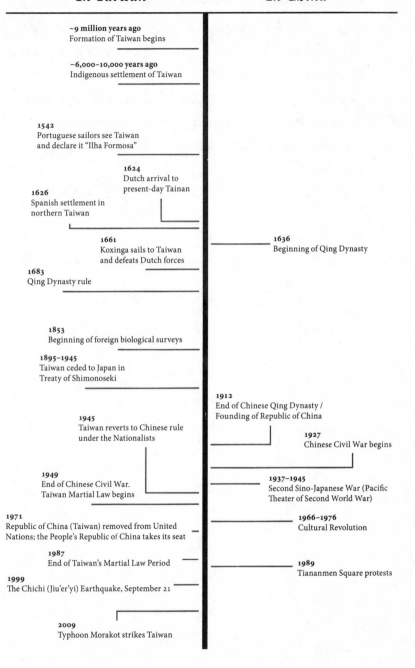

In Taiwan

In China

~9 million years ago
Formation of Taiwan begins

~6,000–10,000 years ago
Indigenous settlement of Taiwan

1542
Portuguese sailors see Taiwan
and declare it "Ilha Formosa"

1624
Dutch arrival to
present-day Tainan

1626
Spanish settlement in
northern Taiwan

1661
Koxinga sails to Taiwan
and defeats Dutch forces

1636
Beginning of Qing Dynasty

1683
Qing Dynasty rule

1853
Beginning of foreign biological surveys

1895–1945
Taiwan ceded to Japan in
Treaty of Shimonoseki

1912
End of Chinese Qing Dynasty /
Founding of Republic of China

1945
Taiwan reverts to Chinese rule
under the Nationalists

1927
Chinese Civil War begins

1949
End of Chinese Civil War.
Taiwan Martial Law begins

1937–1945
Second Sino-Japanese War (Pacific
Theater of Second World War)

1971
Republic of China (Taiwan) removed from United
Nations; the People's Republic of China takes its seat

1966–1976
Cultural Revolution

1987
End of Taiwan's Martial Law Period

1989
Tiananmen Square protests

1999
The Chichi (Jiu'er'yi) Earthquake, September 21

2009
Typhoon Morakot strikes Taiwan

TAIWAN
(REPUBLIC OF CHINA)

East China Sea

Taipei

Keelung

Hsinchu

Huiyao Waterfall

Taiwan Strait

Taichung

Zhuilu Old Road

Shuishe Mountain

Qilai Mountain

Shuiyang Forest

Taijiang National Park

Tainan

Kaohsiung

Qikong Falls

Kenting

Philippine Sea

島

DAO

n. ISLAND

*Islands emerge through movement, through
collision, and through accretion.*

1

I HAVE LEARNED MANY WORDS FOR "ISLAND": isle, atoll, eyot, skerry. They exist in archipelagos or alone, and I have always understood them by their relation to water. The English word "island," after all, comes from the German "aue," from the Latin "aqua," meaning "water." An island is a world afloat; an archipelago is a place pelagic.

The Chinese word for island knows nothing of water. For a civilization grown inland from the sea, the vastness of mountains was a better metaphor: 島 dao ("island," pronounced "to" in Taiwanese) is built from the relationship between earth and sky. The character contains the idea that a bird 鳥 (niao) can rest on a lone mountain 山 (shan).

Taiwan is just eighty-nine miles wide, but in that distance it climbs nearly thirteen thousand feet from sea level. The jump to precipitous peaks creates a wealth of habitats, such that the island sustains a range of forests much vaster than its small footprint. The coasts are muffled with salt- and sun-soaked mangroves, and moving south, thick tropical jungle grows. The wet heat of a tropical rain forest thrums to temperate trees, and their hardwoods climb to pines. Boreal forests—with towering, size-of-a-house cathedral trees—grow up from the middle slopes of the island. Beyond the tree line, the mountains peter out to prairie, cane grasslands widening toward an alpine sky. Like topographical rings on a map, the trees array themselves by elevation.

Born into conflict at the junction of two volcanic arcs, Taiwan is an unstable landmass in perpetual confrontation. Set along the Ring of Fire—the Pacific zone plagued by quakes and eruptions—southeast of China, west of Japan, north of the Philippines, the island marks the border of two tectonic plates: this is known to geologists as a destructive plate boundary. The collision of the Eurasian and Philippine Sea plates forced the island into being some 6 to 9 million years ago, during the Miocene epoch. Such collisions are powerful, with one plate thrust beneath another, raising land from the sea and into the air. But these borders can be devastating, too.

The Central Mountain Range, running some 170 miles, four-fifths of the island's length, and the Hsueh-shan Range, arcing halfway across the island's north, are flanked on either side by faults. The foothills and flatlands to the west wear breakage like errant stitching on a quilt, determining and dividing the landscape. To the east, the Coastal Mountain Range is pressed between fault lines and the sea.

More than two hundred of the island's peaks are higher than three thousand meters, monuments to tectonic change set fast into schist, gneiss, marble, and slate. The mountains are among the youngest in the world, and they continue to shift as the Philippine Sea Plate moves westward at around eighty millimeters a year. Through the forces of orogeny that form great mountain chains, Taiwan's peaks stand taller every day.

Islands transfix us, their mythologies tied as much to their isolation as to imagination. Long-sought Ithaca or the seaport in a tempest, the islands I know from stories can be both real and fanciful; material places of rock and soil, they come laden with the ideological weight of Edens and arcadias, with visions of paradise.

The Chinese coastline is littered with islands close at hand—easy to reach, knowable—but for centuries, those in the distance across the Taiwan Strait or the East China Sea remained treacherous to reach and explore. It is easy to imagine how they might have been idealized, or likewise abhorred, for their distance from Chinese civilization. In Chinese myth, Penglai—described as both a mountain and an island—was the home of the immortals, blessed with cups that never ran dry, with rice bowls that never emptied. In the third century B.C., the first emperor of a unified China sought the mythic island, sailing his ships to the east. It is said that the emperor's emissaries found Japan instead.

But Penglai—蓬萊—is also one of the traditional names for Taiwan. It was for this wealth of natural resources that Qing explorers first ventured to the island that was renowned for its abundance. In 1697, the colonial scribe Yu Yonghe traveled in search of sulfur. In his journey along the coast, led by indigenous guides and servants, he described rice grains the size of beans and island crops providing perhaps twice the harvest of the mainland. Coconuts could be split and used as cups for wine. He wrote that Taiwan's fruit—plentiful but mostly unfamiliar to the voyagers—would spoil on the journey back to the mainland; the island was vital and abundant but entirely unto itself. For those from the continent, these eastern archipelagos were brimming with life, mountains in a turbulent sea. But unlike the immortal islands of myth,

Taiwan belonged to the material realm, a living world on a fault-ridden terrain.

This is a story of that island. And it is also a story of family.

•

LANGUAGES BECOME A HOME. IN ENGLISH, I find my mind, and in German, my present life in Berlin. But my earliest words in childhood were in Mandarin, my mother's tongue. I know them still. 狗 gou ("dog"), 老虎 laohu ("tiger"), 愛 ai ("love"), and especially:

婆

Po

Grandmother.

公

Gong

Grandfather.

Po and Gong had moved from China—from homesteads no one had left in generations—to Taiwan, where they lived for nearly four decades, unable to return to the mainland. They arrived in the years after the Second World War, along with more than 1 million other mainland Chinese when Chiang

Kai-shek's Nationalist (Kuomintang or KMT) government fled to Taiwan at the end of the civil war.

Taiwan had changed hands repeatedly: Though its indigenous inhabitants had lived there for thousands of years, the arrival of the Spanish and the Dutch East India Company in the seventeenth century spurred a continuous scramble for the island. The Dutch and Spanish both set up trading posts on the western shores and were succeeded by Chinese colonists, who held the island for over two centuries. After the First Sino-Japanese War, Japan ruled the island from 1895 until 1945, when it was transferred back to China. When my grandparents arrived, the decades of cultural separation were an even greater gulf to cross.

People like my grandparents and their descendants became known in Taiwan as 外省人 waishengren (literally "people from outside the province," meaning mainlanders), a term so imprecise that even now I wonder how to explain our origins. Our histories stretched across places imprecisely until our borders grew too hazy to define. Eventually, with my mother, my grandparents immigrated to Canada, where I was born. My grandfather, nearing his death, left Canada and returned to Taiwan. I grew older and then moved away myself—first to Britain, where my father is from, and then to Germany, where I made my life as a writer and academic. My mother, sister, and I stumbled over whether to call ourselves Chinese—we weren't from a China that exists any longer—or Taiwanese. No single word can contain the movements that carried our story across waters, across continents.

Names are rarely uncomplicated markers. So often they are born from the snares of conquest, from the declarations and misunderstandings of those who sailed from foreign shores. From China and Japan; from Portugal, Spain, and the Netherlands. Ilha Formosa: Portuguese for "Beautiful Island." Tayouan, an ethnonym taken from a local indigenous settlement. Ryukyu or Liuqiu, the island arc of Okinawa, of which Taiwan marks a geological end. Taiwan is rendered in script as 臺灣 or 台灣, tai for "platform" or "terrace," wan for "bay." A foothold in a churning sea.

Names here are buried and written-over things, erupting from the ground underfoot the way faults emerge from a quake. 中華民國 Zhonghua Minguo, "Republic of China" as the country has been officially known since 1945. Or that incendiary marker, "Taiwan, Province of China."

Disruption is written in the island's stone: forged in movement, scattered with dormant volcanic hills and slopes that rise from sea to sky so swiftly they cannot be captured in a single glance. It is a place that demands time and slow attention but can be undone in a single moment of subterranean trembling.

I was eighteen when my grandfather forgot who I was. I was napping on the sofa at my grandparents' bungalow in Niagara Falls, waiting for my mother to drive us back home. I'd stayed in the bungalow a hundred times before: on school holidays, at weekends, and when my parents would travel for work. Its thick orange carpeting was familiar underfoot. I knew the feel of its light switches in the darkness, where the edges of the smoked-glass dining table protruded, and which of my childhood photographs belonged on which shelf. Mildewed stacks of Chinese newspapers dwelled in the corners, absorbing the polypropylene smell of the VHS tapes of Taiwanese soap operas that towered in the basement. I'd memorized the sounds and smells, the landscape scenes wrought in jade that my grandfather loved, and had helped care for the bonsai tree he kept. I slept comfortably, curled into the summer stickiness of the black leather sofa, until Gong stood at my feet, pointed at me, and spoke in the only language he had left.

那是誰？
Na shi shei?
"Who is that?"

Gong's Alzheimer's had made itself apparent to me, and I began to ask questions. The realization that the past was quickly dissolving gave an urgency to the task of knowing it. I had taken so much of my grandparents' lives for granted, and language had been a barrier. I had stopped going to Saturday Chinese school when I was eight, dreading being the only half-Chinese kid in the classroom as we plowed through the three-hour span of calligraphy and folk songs, so my Mandarin dwindled and faded to its most basic. Our lives together took on a simplified form: my memories of Po and Gong are mostly of the food they cooked.

My father's large family held a kind of gravitational pull. His parents moved from Wales to Canada when my older sister, Nika, and I were young, and with them I felt the warmth of a shared language, of cousins and distant relatives. But we didn't have other family on my mother's side—no aunties or great-grandmothers or cousins to call on. It had always been this way; I thought it was like that for many immigrant families, spread across the world as we were.

I knew that my grandparents had been born in China, but considered Taiwan home. I had a vague sense of why, though I'd visited the island only as an infant. I heard occasional mention of past wars and government leaders, of fighter jets and the ills of communism, but that history was not taught in Canadian schools. When people heard my family was from Taiwan, they would often reply, "Thailand? I love Thai food." I learned to correct them, tactfully and smiling, never wanting to make my frustration known; but I realized, too, how little I knew myself.

To me, Po had simply always been my irascible, difficult grandmother. She squabbled with my mother and father and hardly talked to my grandfather, save in reproach. The energy she spent in spoiling Nika and me—buying us giant teddy bears and Toblerone and Ferrero Rocher chocolates—could shift quickly, and there were times when I kept my distance. She could wound with a word, and often would.

Gong had always been quiet, reading or caring for his plants in a solitary way during his time off from work as a janitor. When I was small, I would visit and watch him mop the floors of the Chef Boyardee canned-pasta factory. The brown-bricked building fascinated me, with its enormous steel machines and the pervasive smell of boiled starch and citrus cleaner. I would watch him clean, quiet as ever, and then beam with childish pride when he bought me a can of beef ravioli. I never questioned how his life had taken him there, long past retirement, dragging a hot mop across the floor of a Canadian factory.

I was twenty-seven when I went to Taiwan for the second time, my first visit since I was a baby. It was 2013. Gong had returned there and died a few years earlier, and my mother and I had gone to visit his remains. He had died alone, his memories wasted. It felt, to us, an irrevocable betrayal, though we'd had no say in what had happened and we couldn't have changed it.

Decades had passed since my mother had emigrated. But the island had called my family back. My mother began to talk about returning for good when she retired. I saw the ways she had tried on a different life on a different continent, and how it bristled speaking a language she'd inherited, asking her children questions in Mandarin and receiving replies in English. We mocked her errors, as children do, and she would reply, "Well, you speak Chinese, then," jokingly, though I sensed a loss in her tone. I saw in Taiwan something of the ways that places draw us in—and sometimes push us away again—and there grew in me an inarticulate longing.

My mother and I spent the better part of that visit wandering overgrown hills and trails outside the cities, in the hot and overgrown forests she had once known, where as a child she had roamed the green sprawl near her home, wandering wet through rice paddies on late afternoons, where she had memorized the plants that sprung vivid from every patch.

We ventured to the south, to Kenting, where she'd spent childhood holidays on the peninsula of coral. We soaked in northern rain in Yangmingshan, and delved into the mist that blanketed Taroko. Those first days in the cloud forest softened me to fog. In the mountains, I saw curtains of growth that clung to the cliffs, draping and enfolding every jagged bone of the mountainside. They petered out into clumps of withered brown stone where rock had not yet relented to root. But spiny trees grew from the holes left by erosion, and vines navigated the smoothed-down faces of the stone. The green was unceasing in its efforts.

It felt as if we were finding in the landscape an expression of this place and our lives beyond my grandfather's death, beyond a past I did not fully understand. I developed a love for these mountains and their forests, a need to return and return again.

I lamented the years we'd stayed away. It wasn't nostalgia—a dangerous thing, if it sees too narrowly—but still, other words could not account for it. Sehnsucht, from my adopted language, German—a yearning for another course, for things that could have been different—perhaps. Hiraeth, from Welsh—a homesickness for a past to which I could not return—came close. There is a Chinese word—鄉情 (xiangqing)—that means "longing for one's native place." But none of them quite fit. Unable to determine my feelings with words, I began to think, perhaps, that whatever force had stitched my grandparents and my mother to this place had caught me, with just a thread at first, and then bound me to it still stronger. My grief was displaced by deep affection. Does regret, by nature, transmute into longing?

I do not think it was a unique desire. I know others who have lost places or relatives, who have taken comfort in returning, as if exercising a muscle memory passed down through the generations. I found a constancy and a comfort in walking the island's hills.

And where I couldn't find words, I fell to other languages: to plants, to history, to landscape. My work as an environmental historian had taught me a great deal about temperate plants and navigating my way through a Canadian pine forest or a European heath with familiarity. In the vast and unrolling woodlands I grew up with in Canada, there is the red flame of autumn, the spare and silent retreat of winter. The pines and maples do their seasonal dance: pollen, senescence, bare branch.

But in Taiwan I found myself botanically adrift, as unsure of the trees as I was of the ferns that sprouted from windowsills. Taiwan's plants are too many to name.

A green washes itself over Taiwan's hillsides, a mottled, deep hue that reminds me more of lake than of land, of darkened waterweed more than tree. The green rolls out on the horizon, glinting with occasional light, but more often steaming with the low-hanging clouds that cling to the border between hillside and sky. That verdant hue is unlike any other I know.

Taiwan's hills form a natural boundary between the cities and the mountains. Camphor laurels, peeling elms, charcoal trees, banyans, and sugar palms are overrun with the unfurling of ferns beyond number, with giant taros that stand gaping under heavy rain. The parasols of the eight-fingered *Diplofatsia* reach their hands to the sky. Their many greens stand layered, saturated, and deepened.

The island holds both migrant and endemic species. There are plants that came from the continent, carried by birds or other animals, by air or by the land bridge that once filled the Taiwan Strait when sea levels were lower, many ages ago. Some came from the island chain to the east—Japan—while others floated atop the southern seas, sprouting on the shores. There are newer plants that arose only here, a quarter of them evolved in isolation on their island home. In

Taiwan's plants I saw both movement and change: species adapting to climate, to altitude, to soil.

I met mimosa that curled at my touch. *Dendrocalamus latiflorus*, Latin for "tree reed": sweet bamboos whose tall heads swayed. In my visits, I came to know them by walking, by crouching low to the ground to catch a scent, and by training the lens of my camera on their distant reaches.

I searched books for a guide. I found in the works of nineteenth-century British geographers a strange vision of the island. Their accounts of Taiwan's inner reaches held a trace of terror—the plants too foreign, the forests too thick. They wrote of the island as beautiful yet threatening, a wilderness overgrown; the sublimity of extremely high mountains found an analogue just as readily in darkened woods. John Thomson, a photographer and fellow of the Royal Geographical Society, wrote of softly beautiful mountain scenery cut through with gigantic forests, where "climbing parasitic plants passing from tree to tree formed a chaos like the confusion of ropes on a Chinese junk." These portrayals mingled beauty with fear, with curiosity and exoticism, occasionally with disgust. Though written in English, I struggled to find in them a language I could share.

But this was the green my mother grew up with.

She told me the Mandarin names of plants I had no reference for, passed on from my grandfather to her: 鳳凰木 fenghuang mu (phoenix or flame trees) and 芭蕉 bajiao, a fibrous, inedible species of banana; her childhood through the names of trees. I turned their names over in my mouth, stretching their shapes into my mind, and found in them a longing to remember the things I had not known.

2

TAIPEI WAS A CITY THAT BELONGED TO MY childhood imagination. Built of words spoken quietly to me by my mother, its streets were paved with her longings. The air was made of memories. In this place, Taipei was a single hillside, a school at its crest and a tenement block at its base. A packed-dirt road cut a straight line between them, bustling with street-food sellers in carts that looked uncannily like the Toronto hot dog vendors of my youth. There was no wind, and there were no trees. The light was yellow, and the only smell was that of the choudoufu my mother missed most after leaving Taiwan.

"But does it really smell like poo?" I would ask her, having never smelled choudoufu before.

"Not at all! It smells delicious," she would reply, tucking me into bed.

"Then why is it called stinky tofu?"

She would shrug, smiling as if a morsel of that memory had just passed her lips.

Every day as a schoolgirl my mother would linger on the hillside buying snacks, avoiding going home after school. She loved to eat, so her face was rounder then, her body plumper, like the one black-and-white photograph I had seen from that time. She bought tofu and spring onion pancakes and sugarcane juice with handfuls, I imagine, of silver coins.

By the time she would make it home, it was sundown. The apartment was green-gray and dark, with bars over the windows and plants everywhere. Dust hung suspended in the air. She would sneak in quietly to avoid getting into trouble. But she wasn't quiet enough. My grandmother had been angry that she had taken so long to come home. Worse, she was getting a bit fat. Po waved the meat cleaver. There were angry words, and my mother was bundled into her bedroom. The door locked.

She told me about Taipei in fragments, and sometimes I wondered if this was all she could remember. Taipei in 1960 was home to nearly 1 million people, but the past she reconstructed for me was a small picture: my grandparents, herself, and a wok full of deep-fried tofu. An entire city reduced to a single road of street vendors.

In adulthood, my time in Taiwan relieved me of

this naive picture. I found a city unfolding from the flatlands of the western coast, a web of aging concrete apartment complexes towered over by glassy high-rises. Elevated highways spiraled, ensnaring the scooters that pollinated the thoroughfares with fumes. Tiled walls were caked with algae, and on every old building the signs of nature's tenacity showed themselves: ferns growing from brick-thick ledges, flowers springing skyward from the joints of old awnings. Tucked into a river basin with leaf-laden slopes on all sides, the city center was flat and uniform. The stark, lonely hillside of my childhood imagining was nowhere to be seen. Instead, the green hills that surround the river basin were the dark background to my every movement.

I walked Taipei's streets—with my mother and alone—in search of an anchor, my map a jumble of transliterations and characters pressed into the too-small spaces of the lines of roads. I wanted to learn the island by its landmarks, the way my mother had once done, but the open stretches of rice paddy and field that she had once known had become part of the city, with broad avenues and famous skyscrapers.

Once, we found one of the old city gates stranded in the middle of a roundabout, and my mother knew immediately where she was, despite the new road. A hundred meters beyond it, she was lost again.

I found myself drawn to the island's backbone. In forests and on mountains, the urgency of time receded and the pacing minutes I'd grown accustomed to in the city stretched molten until they evaporated, small and inconsequential things in the face of arboreal and lithic time. It was on trails that I ceased to check my phone, turning my attention instead to the multitudes that arrayed themselves at my feet: the compression of ages, packed tight by many walkers, the patient growth of moss on weathered stones, and, when I was very high up beyond the tree line or on some rocky outcrop, the layered stones that tell the story of a mountain. I moved from the human timescale of my family's story through green and unfurling dendrological time, to that which far exceeds the scope of my understanding: the deep and fathomless span of geological time.

Many of my days roaming these slopes were shrouded in trees, and on the occasions that I rose beyond them, I found myself in cloud. The tree line here was a good thousand meters higher than on the European mountains I'd grown used to, up to 3,500 meters altitude, a remarkable thing when traveling the island's short span from sea level to the mountains. The geology of Taiwan tells a complex tale of emergence into air and compaction over time, of magmatic flows and stark coral limestone thrust from salt water. But on shattered slopes—made worse by tree clearance, mining, and mono-crop plantations—I saw the damage wrought by typhoons and quakes, the slow steadiness of stone diminished to scree, the tracks of graveled mud left in the flow of landslides. Mountains could be rattled all too quickly, their timelines fractured in mere moments.

·

IT IS 2017, AND I HAVE COME ALONE WITH A plan to stay for three months to work on my Mandarin, to write, and above all, to hike. It is October. I've taken an apartment in the east of Taipei, the last house on the last lane before the mountains curve along the southern edge of the sprawl. In the shadow of that lithic presence, it is a home akin to the one in my mother's memories. An old concrete building— tiled in white that has grown thick with mildew— with bars framing the few small windows and jade plastic awnings reaching out from the balconies on every floor. It is dark inside; the glassy towers of new construction have not yet come to this stretch of road.

From here, I watch the streetlights blink into life, casting a yellow gleam on the asphalt. A dog sleeps outside the temple next door, curling amid the scalene patches of light that fall from the windows above. In time he will come to know me. The scent of choudoufu carries down the lane from the hawker who sets up his stall each night next to the 7-Eleven on the corner.

It is easy to see the traces of the city around me in the snares of polyethylene bags strewn by the roadside, discarded umbrellas, bald tires and spare pylons, and scooters lined up for the evening. But there is more than these human relics: leathered leaves of *Osmanthus* and fig, the frilled skyline of acacias and banyans looming in shadow. Cicadas sing a susurrus in hiding, amid the swell of growth that patterns the end of the lane, the bracken and grass and the small inklings of banana leaf reaching above the asphalt's fringe.

Beyond the lane, the green rises into the hills. Xiangshan—Elephant Mountain—is one in a series of four small peaks stretching across the southeastern edge of Taipei. Together, they make up the Si Shou Shan (四獸山, Four Beasts Mountains), forest-covered and undulating, sleeping beyond the edge of the Taipei Basin's flat valley. Reaching only a modest elevation, the smaller slopes seem a gesture of welcome from the mountain's heights. From their vantage, I hope to see the low-slung flatness of the basin, to sense the geological grammar of the cityscape below.

This is a young-enough place that uncertainty still prevails: geologists and seismologists continue work to explain the intricacies of the island's formation, and the scooped-out center of the Taipei Basin garners steady attention. Early twentieth-century studies surmised that the basin had formed when a volcanic eruption led to the collapse of the subsurface, the layer of rock and soil beneath ground. Others have suggested that the basin may be a drained lake, dammed by the spoil of volcanic eruption. Still others have thought it a fallen hanging wall, the upper block of land remaining when a fault line fractured the ground. But today it is believed to exist, in part, because of the flexure of the earth's crust as orogeny—mountain building—has taken place, through the slow-motion crumpling of the ground ahead as mountain ranges have advanced. The land dipped, the way a small valley forms at the base of a wave rushing forward.

Roaming into the hills surrounding the basin, it is more humid than on the streets. Steps mark the early reaches of the trail, and I take them two at a time, childlike, scarcely watching my footing on the aging stones, which are worn down as much by weather as the tread of climbers. A short distance up, I begin to peel off layers of clothing. It has been raining, and small puddles have formed at the edge of the path like tiny moats between the walkers and the forest.

The first plateau slows my pace, a more leisurely

gait made possible by the widening of the trail. The scent of soil hovers above the hill, released by rain and by the consecutive footsteps of hikers churning the stone and ground. Mosquitoes rise like pollen from the clusters of damp growth. Taro leaves as wide as newspapers unfurl, their water-filled mouths open to the sky, green pools suspended in the air. The younger leaves are a lime color, curled upright as if pointing my way on the trail.

At the peak of Xiangshan, where a number of boulders cluster at the precipice, groups gather to take selfies. I roam onward to where the hill slips away and a view of the city opens outward: a checkered beige of tower blocks speckled with dark windows, the metal-blue glass of Taipei 101, once the world's tallest skyscraper, stretching above them.

Hushan, Tiger Mountain, is to the east, its trail-head emerging near the end of my road. On quiet days I amble its slopes, idly, umbrella held tightly over my body to stave off the rain that falls from the canopy. It is here that I wander above the city my family called home and that I watch the gray streets rolling out into the hills, the city expanding at a rate faster than the movement of mountains.

3

MY GRANDMOTHER DIED A DECADE AFTER MY grandfather. I had long believed that her death would mark not simply the end of her life, but of the possibility of knowing a past for my mother's family. Our relatives had been lost—either in death or by loss of contact—after the end of the Chinese Civil War. My mother became the sole inheritor of their history, the only person of our maternal family that remained.

What Po left behind stood towered on tabletops, tucked into closets and corners, dusted atop chair seats. In the years after my grandfather's death she had moved to an apartment block near my mother's home and battened herself within its walls. She allowed no one in to help her and gave us no authority to care for her. So when she died, my mother found monoliths of paper littering the apartment: bills, letters, documents, and newspapers. Old food, chipped dishes, and bottles of medicine lined the shelves. Perpetually suspicious that we or others were stealing, Po had built a home among these yellowed memorials to a lifetime past. Like an archaeologist set to a dig, my mother was left to dismantle and catalogue the enclosed world Po had built.

She took a week off work to sort through it all, sifting the newspapers, bills, and scrawled notes trying to find Po's will, pension information, bank accounts, and Gong's death certificate, which could not be unearthed.

She bagged up old clothes, thick with the scent of camphor, took pictures of heirlooms she planned to set aside for my sister and me, and spent hours scrubbing the filthy corners that had gone unkept in Po's near-blindness. I was an ocean away, so she texted me photos and questions from time to time, asking if I wanted old things like a pair of sunglasses or a painted vase. With no one else to send things on to, anything my sister and I didn't want, she said conclusively, would go to the Salvation Army.

In that clutter my mother made two discoveries. The first, a slim envelope from her father, sealed some decades earlier. It was intended, she could see from the label, to be given to her for safekeeping after his death.

The other was a phone bill, innocuous perhaps, except that it listed a series of calls to Taiwan and China. Who was Po calling? Three weeks later, my mother rang to tell me the news. She had dialed one of the numbers. The call connected us to family we'd believed lost forever.

•

ON THAT FIRST TRIP BACK, MY MOTHER AND I took a frill-curtained coach south along the coastal highway. On the Hengchun Peninsula, at the island's southern tip, shelves of pockmarked coral dried inland; the large, brittle grains mingled with the soil of the hills. The slopes down south are lower than elsewhere, lazily unrolling toward the sea, an easeful geology.

Off-season traffic lolled around the clutch of holiday towns that had grown up out of the shoreline. We disembarked at Kenting and found our way to the empty beach. At three in the afternoon, there seemed to be no one around but us.

December winds blew down from the north: the 落山風 luoshanfeng (literally "wind that falls down from the mountains"), which surges each winter over the south of Taiwan from the slopes where the backbone range terminates. The wind blew hard from the hills, gusting between the spare buildings, out over the gray beach where my mother braced herself between the wind and the waves. She was combing for treasure.

The sea had not merely buried the things that once belonged to air. It was a place of building, where beneath the waves the calcite dance of coral accretion unfolded. In time, these limestone remnants of the sea were lifted and brought to dry in the light and heat, laid amid the crumpled waste of sediments shaved from the advancing mountains. But such movements occurred impossibly slowly, unseen; the beach grew languorous in winter, and the shoreline on which we stood seemed an unlikely candidate for such dramatic change.

My mother, in her sixties, moved across the beach with a childlike lack of urgency, her attention absorbed in the task of beachcombing. Every so often, she would stand up from her huddled position, a gleaming purple prize in her hands. She gathered the remnants of the sea in her pockets, which bulged with their irregular forms: smooth-washed sea glass and scrubbed stones. The occasional polished and gleaming spindle cone or cowrie shell presented itself, but most of what she found was softened coral, sanded down by a lifetime in the tides. She assembled and admired them over the afternoon, leaving mounds of stone and shell in the slack of the waves. One of them she kept: a purple clamshell the size of a coin.

Mom had been there many times before, and our return was an indulgence of her memories. She'd vacationed here with Po and Gong in the 1960s, when the white sand of Baisha Bay seemed a remoter place, its pale crescent receding into the South China Sea. She spent that day in Kenting as she had as a ten-year-old girl, losing herself in the trifles of the tideline.

I watched her, skittering from incoming waves like a sandpiper searching for clams, and saw something of the past in her. In Taiwan, though so much had changed, my mother became a person with a topographic history, a person set into the scene in which she believed she belonged. In my childhood, I never saw that in her: In forty years of life in Canada, she had never rooted to the place and got lost easily. On her commutes in rush-hour traffic, she did not stray from her prescribed path. But on the beach I realized that she'd carried something of the island in her the entire time, molecularly, absorbed the way water swells beneath the skin. Tracing her way across the shore, she worked the place into her bones once more.

•

A FEW DAYS AFTER FINDING GONG'S LETTER, MY mother called me again. She had pried the envelope open to find twenty thinning sheets of loose-leaf paper, scrawled with Chinese script. It was my grandfather's handwriting, faded with age. Letters from Gong, undated, unsent. Tentatively, having not seen her father's writing in a decade, she began to read the pages.

An autobiography of his life, looping around and repeating his story, it traced his movement from China, as a child born in 1919 amid the turbulence of the May Fourth Movement, which protested China's poor returns from the Paris Peace Conference and the Treaty of Versailles, the failure of Chinese diplomats to represent the nation's interests, and the subsequent handover of Chinese territory to the Japanese. He grew up amid the cultural, intellectual, and political changes in the years following those protests, during which the Chinese Communist Party was formed. The bulk of the letter centered on the Second Sino-Japanese War, on his time as a pilot for the Flying

Tigers. It followed his years in Taiwan, where he was an instructor for the Republic of China's Air Force, and then it ended abruptly in the middle of a sentence, unanchored in any time. Perhaps he had begun writing to remind himself of who he was. The story was just a series of fragments, circled and repeated— pieces of his life told to no one before, pressed to paper, and perhaps forgotten by him soon after writing.

The grip of his disease had already wasted his memories by then.

My mother let me have them. She posted a copy to me, annotating the script with translations and insights known only from the intimacy of her relationship with him: she knew the names of friends or politicians and generals to whom he'd referred, and could sense when he'd recalled something in error, swapping a name or a place for another from the distance of decades.

In my hands, the pages brought out a choking kind of grief. I could barely hold them without crying. Their existence broke my heart doubly, for I could not read them. His handwritten scrawl was far beyond my abilities. Did he begin on the right of the page, writing top to bottom? Sometimes I'd seen him write from the left. When could he have written them? And why—why—had the letter been kept from us?

My earliest memory of Gong is from a photograph. It is my second birthday, and I am leaning over the candles of my birthday cake, a chocolate-frosted train with pineapples for wheels. Gong sits on a lawn chair behind in a white cardigan and a red polo shirt. He is silver-haired and smiling, eyes creased and skin browned in the summer sun, sitting half out of the frame. It is just a fragment of his image, but I hold it close, a time when all of him was there.

Alzheimer's, I think, is a form of haunting. It possesses the people we love, takes them away in stages, devouring memory, life, personality. As the disease progresses, the proteins that gather in the brain begin to form plaque around nerve cells, structures that once transported nutrients collapse, and the brain tissue shrinks. First short-term then long-term memories disappear. The people we know fade as though gradually stepping out of a picture.

His was a slow leaving. He resisted it. In his letter were parts I had never seen of the smiling, quiet man who had made spaghetti or folded dumplings, who had danced giddy with me in stacked shoes at holiday parties. They were parts left in Taiwan, pieces he shared with no one, things he had lost in China. They belonged to those places and to the person he had been when all of him was there.

I asked my mother to write out the names of our family. On a scrap of paper, she shaped three names:

The first was my grandfather's, Tsao Chung-chin, his name topped with 山 shan, the mountain radical. My grandmother's name, Yang Kwei-lin, was replete with trees: the wood radical 木 mu stood scattered through its syllables. The third name was my own, my surname crowned with its arboreal root 李 li (for "plum"), and my Chinese name, Jie-ke. A stone washed clean by water.

4

THE STORY OF A PLACE—LITHIC, LIVING, AND forgotten—can be found in maps and what they include or leave out. Before the sixteenth century, Taiwan was considered by the Chinese to be a wilderness well beyond the bounds of their empire. Very little was known of the island across the treacherous Black Ditch, as the Taiwan Strait was affectionately called.

It has been said that the Portuguese passed the island on a journey to Japan in 1542 and dubbed it "Ilha Formosa." In the years that followed, efforts to chart and colonize the landscape began in earnest, and maps of the region convey the history of those turbulent years. There are sixteenth-century Spanish maps, like the one produced by Hernando de los Ríos Coronel in 1597, intended to position the island among Spain's colonial holdings in the Philippines. Taiwan on this map is not yet given true shape: it is a crude, rectangular-shaped thing, its northern bays exaggerated to emphasize their military and commercial import to the Spanish. The Dutch maps that followed in the seventeenth century detail the coastlines of their central island port and the Pescadores (now known as the Penghu Islands) off to the west.

In a 1700 Qing map, the perspective is tilted to the horizontal, drawn from the map reader's view—the view of migrants leaving China for Taiwan—as if seeing the island from a lookout at sea. The green foothills and eastern peaks are hazed in blue in the distance. In the 山水 shanshui-style (literally "mountain water") maps of this period, which take their cue from traditional landscape painting, the rivers run to sea like arteries, and the mountain spine forms a horizon. The world beyond those mountains remained unmapped. An eighteenth-century French map sums up the difficulty presented by Taiwan's landscape: the flatlands of the west—by then colonized by the Spanish, Dutch, and Chinese—could be mapped, but the mountains of the precipitous east coast remained inaccessible. "Toute cette Coste est très peu connue" ("Of this coast, very little is known"), claims Jacques-Nicolas Bellin's 1763 map. In all the colonial renderings, there is a common feature: the backbone range of mountains marked the edge of cartographic knowledge.

Little was known—but much, and little positive, conjectured—of Taiwan's indigenous peoples, who had made their home on the island for some five thousand years until, with the arrival of foreign powers, many of them were forced into either assimilation or the difficult terrain of the high mountains. In leaving out the mountains and the eastern coast, the maps depicted both topography and a view that indigenous people remained outside civilization. Beyond these maps, such blinkered visions of the island's past now exist mostly in the records of travelers.

I once spent a few weeks absorbed in reading about that washed-away coastline in *Taiwan's Imagined Geography*, a 2004 visual-cultural history by the Taiwanese American academic Emma Jinhua Teng. Though small numbers of Han Chinese had fished or traded on the island since the early 1600s, it was only in the mid-seventeenth century that Taiwan became a frontier for the Chinese and an island in often violent contention. In 1661 and 1662, Ming loyalists forced from the mainland besieged and took the island from the Dutch East India Company, which had itself made efforts to domesticate the land and suppress the indigenous islanders. In the decades that followed, increasing numbers of Han Chinese came from the southern coast of the mainland, most settling land for agriculture. And in time, Qing troops arrived. In 1683, Taiwan was absorbed into the Chinese empire.

Perhaps it was the book's title—its harkening of an *imagined* geography—that had caught my attention as I flitted through the stack of hardcovers the librarian had handed over. Taiwan and its past had inhabited my imagination for most of my life. My family had arrived there centuries after the period covered in the book, but still, ours and the island's identity—and our relationship to China especially—was troubled. The past presented a mirror: much of Teng's book focuses on the images and maps from when Taiwan transitioned from being cast as a miasmic wilderness beyond the seas of China to a valuable part of the empire. This shift was influenced in no small part by the wealth of natural resources on the island. It was the moment the Chinese first laid claim to Taiwan. Of course, as Teng is quick to note, the success of the current "One China" view claiming Taiwan as part of Chinese territory can be "measured by the disappearance from the Chinese collective memory of the pre-Qing conviction that Taiwan was 'beyond the pale.'"

From Teng, I moved to the travelogues of Yu Yonghe. In 1696, the Qing imperial gunpowder stores exploded; the depleted stocks created enormous demand for the wealth of sulfur to be found in Taiwan's volcanic north. In 裨海紀遊 Bihai Jiyou (*Small Sea Travel Diaries*) Yu documented his journey from Xiamen, on China's southern shore, to what is now Tainan. From that newly claimed Chinese harbor, he traveled north in search of natural resources. Yu followed the coast, fording the wide rivers that ran down from the mountains to the strait, documenting the island's flora and fauna, and gave troubling but detailed descriptions of Chinese colonial efforts to "subdue" the indigenous population.

Yu combined verse with prose narrative, flitting from the pearls of light and color splashed by an oar in a dark night's sea—bioluminescent algae, I thought, reading on—to an account of how the Chinese had defeated the Dutch colonists at Tainan. The island was absorbed into the empire grudgingly—because it was needed—but remained, in every way, a remote place.

Today, maps continue to show Taiwan tangled in mystery. The nation occasionally wears a veil of gray; unrecognized by so much of the world, like many disputed places, its status is not a given. But it is as real a place as any. On survey maps—contour maps, seismic hazard maps, geological surveys, bird migrations, forest distribution, and vegetation charts—I've found its materiality set to paper.

In Taiwan, fault lines craze the ground. One map has a list of geohazards and a pile of statistics on Taiwan's natural disasters; another—a seismicity map—has the appearance of a Jackson Pollock painting, only the splatters are denser, set to overwhelm. Having grown up in eastern Canada, where the greatest threat was usually a snowstorm, the turbulence of the island holds for me a certain macabre fascination. My mother's childhood was punctuated by storms and quakes: the swell of the typhoon and an occasional rumbling beneath her feet. She has long repeated what I had believed to be hyperbole as if it were a mantra: "Every day, somewhere in Taiwan, there is an earthquake." In fact, according to a study by the weather service, the island experiences more than fifteen thousand quakes a year, nearly a thousand of which can be felt by people. When I'm in Taiwan, I keep a tracking app on my phone, set to follow every quake above 1.0 on the magnitude scale. The dangers are many: earthquakes, landslides, coastal erosion, land subsidence, volcanic eruption. They are tensions that I cannot fathom.

When earthquakes come, or typhoons sweep across the island, landslides will often follow. Where humans have cleared the land for timber or mined the mountains for gravel, the slopes will flow freely. But in places and in time, their devastation is allayed by trees: the root structures of the forests help stitch the mountains back together. The earth and forest are concomitant things, the trees in need of the right altitude and soil, the ground holding itself together in a web of roots.

From a distance, Taiwan takes the shape of a sweet potato, growing long at its southern tip. On a standard digital map, the landscape appears innocuous: the peaks that form the island's crown are only subtle deviations from the flatlands of the west. But adding terrain to the map, the contrast sharpens. A band of rock forms on the virtual terrain. With a map's satellite view, the deep green body of the island's mountains and foothills presses hard against the ligature of roads and pale farmland in the west. A small place already, so much of Taiwan is given to wilderness and altitude. Seventy-five percent of the land is on a slope, and nearly 60 percent is covered in forest.

The Tropic of Cancer cuts through the midpoint of the island. It is an unseen border, but known to the life that inhabits this place: what is damp mist in the north evaporates into the scorched light of the south. Humidity reigns over all, but the south is hotter, with parched and arid sweeps of mudstone dried into jagged teeth. On islands, as on mountains, the weather shifts on a whim.

•

ON THAT FIRST VISIT AFTER MY GRANDFATHER died, my mother and I had been tracing our way through the southernmost jut of the island, winding the coral-strewn route uphill to where the tip of Taiwan could be seen touching the sea. The forest grew thickly there, a short distance inland from the salt of the shore, and the humidity hung heavy. With green-glossed leaves and aerials over everything, the region felt vastly different from the forests I knew well. The trees were heavy-slung with the lazy shapes of lianas dangling from the branches. Every so often in a clearing, we'd find a looking-glass tree, its buttress roots like pale batwings propping the base of the mangrove, its shape a bizarre reflection of its funhouse name. The tree seemed to belong to an inverted fantasy world, with roots braced perpendicular to the ground, exposed to the air and tall enough to reach a child's height up the trunk, a visible reminder of the vast worlds contained beneath the soil, beneath all the other trees.

The thought of my grandfather hung there, between us, amid the fig trees. I knew my mother's mind was on him whenever we went south—his ashes were not far away, in Kaohsiung—and there weren't words that could salve his absence. She dreamed of him often, she had told me, but in her dreams he was always a ghost, hovering near the ceiling. I didn't tell her that I dreamed of him too, but the scene was always in his darkened room, him perched at the end of the single bed, hands on his knees, silent. Instead, I clasped her hand every so often, hoping the pulse of my palm might convey our shared grief.

There is a motif in Chinese myth that transmutes and shapeshifts depending on the tale and the teller. The "sky ladder" could be a mountain, but at other times it was a rope, a rainbow, or occasionally a cobweb. In my favorite tales, the ladder is a tree, impossibly high, a bridge between the earth and the heavens. What might I see at the crown of such a tree? The tree spanned the distance between mortality and immortality, the profane and the sacred. Climbing it was a feeble grasp toward godliness. I thought of my mother's dream and wondered what Gong had known of the sky, of height. He had been a pilot, after all. He had never had need of such a ladder.

A song cut through the woods, a sweet-toned trill that rippled on the rustle of the banyan leaves. I glanced up to see a small flock of white-masked, black-mustached birds flitting from tree to tree. Their wings glistened in the afternoon light, bellies quivering with the staccato, pitchy tune they piped without end. I settled beneath the trees and watched them, Styan's bulbuls. Endemic to the island, while they are common in the south, they are disappearing elsewhere, edged out of their habitats by construction, cities, and encroachment by other mainland species. Already gone from the northeast, they are found only on this peninsula and the eastern coastal mountains. But here they gather in busy flocks, tittering despite the threats, with a wholehearted mirth in their music.

A short walk uphill, the scent of crushed leaf and rainfall permeated the air. The dusty peaks of limestone coral smelled of dried chalk mingled with the woody scent of the banyan aerials creeping over them. The aerials wound their way into the crevices and pools of shadow, and the trees were just as delicate, hanging precariously atop the fissured outcrops. Banyan roots secrete an acid to erode the coral, enabling their near-acrobatic perches on the rock walls.

Among them hung the leathered green-gray of musk ferns and other clutching, epiphytic growths from the trees, and along the paths I saw fine fingers of maidenhair ferns. Having risen from the sea, the ground in the forest was uneven, climbing at once to precipitous cliffs here and then to sunken trenches there, with caves burrowing beneath the damp soil. Stalactites dripped in the darkness of the earth, but we could only peer down toward their caves filled from winter storms with clouded pools of rain.

We clambered up the hillside, past branches occupied and guarded by brown-fuzzed macaques, silent and watchful. The hum of insects could be picked out from the forest noise only when I focused, training both my eyes and ears to spot them amid the green. Sound preceded sight of the bumblebee—a drone from which they take their Latin name, *Bombus*— which emerged enormous among the delicacy of violet flowers. The electricity of cicadas faded to the background as I listened, watching the bee's clumsy flight from blossom to blossom.

At the end of the steady uphill path, we reached the cleft in the rock known as One-Line Sky. A crack in the tableland rent open by quakes—just wide enough for a person to pass through—ambled through the coral, a single bright strip of sky visible above the trench. It seemed, on first glance, like a corridor to another world, to something elemental and eternal rather than simply the other side of the hill. Sunk down into the mortal world of stone and soil, its walls reached toward the heavens. I gazed vertically to the vast ceiling of the world, and with one hand pressed to rough-worn walls and the other clasped in my mother's, we ventured through that narrow passage.

•

WITH THE FOUNDING OF GEOGRAPHICAL SOCIeties, botanical gardens, and scientific groups in Europe in the late eighteenth and early nineteenth centuries, there emerged a strong impetus for exploration concomitant with colonialism. It would take some decades for efforts to gather pace in East Asia. Exploration, in part, then became a process of exchange: China was opened to Western scientists in the last half of the nineteenth century, and so too was Japan, with travelers returning samples to the collections and botanical gardens of Europe or working with local surveyors to gain a grasp of the vast lands of the Asian continent. Within years, Chinese and Japanese branches of a range of sciences—cartography, geology, botany, zoology—began to emerge and thrive, with their scientists venturing to Kew, Berlin, Paris, and Edinburgh to survey and study lands and scientific collections distant from their own.

By the 1860s, British scientists were working the island into the Western cultural imagination by traveling to Taiwan alongside the Chinese gazetteers, who for centuries had conducted local surveys, often in traditional Chinese cartographic styles. But as the workings of government began to demand the mathematically grounded mapping style of the West, the process of scientific exchange explicitly served political and cultural aims. In cataloguing territory, mapmaking was a tool of colonial governance. The difficult terrain of Taiwan's mountains became a vital target: first, under the Qing administration in the late nineteenth century, and then, under Japanese rule.

In this same period, islands became an ideal object of biological study. They had long transfixed poets and writers and informed mythologies, but their hold on science was just as potent. Such famous isles come quick to mind: the Galápagos Islands, Darwin's muse; Madagascar, beloved by botanists. They were and remain of curious fascination.

Islands can form in a multitude of ways: as land masses attached to continents before becoming encircled by water; at sea, risen from the depths of the ocean by forces tectonic or volcanic; or as accumulated barriers of sand, coral, or glacial remnants. We speak of islands of waste—though the trash vortex does not have the density of ground—and these unseen places enter our collective dreaming of the sea and its familiars, kelp and plastic, intermingled. Still other islands are made in our time: artificial islands, like those military installations hunkered along the coast of China, facing Taiwan, and the contested islands in the South China Sea.

What islands offer to science is as incalculable as their coastlines: species endemism—when a species is unique to a particular place, having adapted in isolation—is a common feature of islands. Many therefore make a contribution to global biodiversity that is disproportionate to their landmass. Think of the character for "island," the single bird on the lone mountaintop: 島. It is on islands that life most strays from the continents. "Isolation," after all, takes its root from the Latin word for island: insula.

Of more than four thousand vascular plant species on Taiwan, more than a thousand are endemic. More than 60 percent of mammals on the island occur nowhere else—the Formosan black bear, deep in the Yushan ranges, or the Formosan macaques, clumsily strutting throughout the south. Nearly half the amphibians and a fifth of birds, like Styan's bulbuls, are unique to this place. On mountain ranges, in particular, the rate of endemism increases: though the number of different species decreases with elevation, as the air thins and grows cold, the singularity of those species increases. Life-forms arrange themselves in these ways. Swinhoe's pheasants and shrill-voiced flamecrests flicker in the middle ranges. Long-lived Formosan cypresses steady themselves on gentle slopes, and montane angelicas frill the thin-aired plateaus.

The range can be dramatic: forest surveys are ringed and banded things that follow the growth of mountains. Oaks and laurels cling to the lower slopes, with cypresses making their languid growth in the damp middle ranges. Above the fog are hemlock and endemic fir, growing upward until snow dusts the shrubs of the highest peaks. With a changing climate and a warming world, for many species there is little place to migrate but skyward. Tree lines creep ever higher, and the realm of the cold-loving species shrinks. Bound to the summits, these species can live a lonely life. And in this way, mountains become islands of their own.

•

BURIED WITHIN THE FOLDS OF THE YELLOWED
envelope, my grandfather's letter felt surprisingly
thin. Unfolding it, I lifted it to the light, so that the
handwriting appeared backlit in glowing rows of parallel script, a landscape on a vertical lined page. It
wasn't much, perhaps twenty pages, but it was all that
remained of Gong. Unsure of touching them, thin
and brittle as they were, I dusted my fingers over the
words, their pen marks deep-set in the page.

There were words I recognized—大 da ("big,"
a person with its arms stretched wide), 媽 ma
("mother," given its meaning from "woman" 女 and
its sound from "horse" 馬), 口 kou ("mouth")—their
ideal forms scrawled as misshapen shadows. I had
to squint to read them, one at a time, stranded in a
crowd I didn't recognize. I stopped at one: 哥哥 gege
(a mouth and a man) rendered with the old radical for
nail (丁), stacked and repeated like an anchor. *Older
brother.* My grandfather was an older brother, and it
was to his sister that he addressed his letter.

He had never spoken to me of his family, beyond
the refrain, repeated by my mom, that he'd learned
to cook at his mother's side. His love had felt total,
unequivocal to me, a small child. He had pressed his
whole palm to my face in affection, and had always
let me help feed his pet turtle, Xiao Wugui, using

a miniature spoon saved from a McDonald's coffee. When his illness became too much to manage, he'd given me the turtle, a red-eared slider the size of a tablespoon. I kept it in my bedroom, a reminder of Gong's love. Now, almost thirty years after Gong first brought him home, the little turtle still grows.

In that single word—gege, "older brother"—an entire life appeared, the possibility of knowing Gong as a child and as a man, more of him than I had ever known.

I had the letter translated and then read it line by line, comparing the characters he'd written to the words typed into English. A work of excavation, of unearthing meaning and context from the lines, my reading stretched out over many days. I took the pages paragraph by paragraph, as if setting the limits of a survey plot, words and names the samples of my search. My mother's notes put pieces in context, and I turned to her marginalia to find relatives she had never met but whose names she had known and historical dates she had memorized as a schoolgirl. Others still were obscure: place names and geographies unknown to us, in a China that no longer exists, from the years when my grandfather was a child.

The letter was disjointed and repetitious: unlike the lithic record geologists find underfoot, Gong's writing had no chronology. The past appeared out of context and out of order, paragraphs out of place. It could be made sense of only when broken into pieces, reemerging in a new linear arrangement. I read it both ways, enclosed in the brambled path of memory and chronologically, identifying the gaps that spanned months or decades. There were stories to which he returned repeatedly, in identical words, like a pilot circling for landing. I marked out the dates and places on a map: the village of his childhood now a rectilinear sprawl, the homes he adopted by necessity. I searched his words for the substrata of a changed land.

THE EARTH WAS PATTERNED RED AND BROWN. She had watched it from the porthole of the plane, waiting in silence as a geometric patchwork became fields cut for harvest and the arboreal carpet sharpened to individual trees. Sugar maples, red oaks, and pines. Suburbs scattered out in all directions, and through them cut a snaking vein of concrete, dotted with cars. Flat, everywhere was flat. The ground rushed up to meet the landing gear, and then all she saw was gray, cloaking the bare ground and low buildings, sending a dusty smell through the air.

This is how I imagine it. On October 13, 1974, Thanksgiving Sunday, my mother arrived in Canada. My grandfather, who had moved a few months earlier, was waiting to pick her up.

She told me about the drive from the airport, her disbelief at the vastness of it all. Immigration was not something she had planned: she had just turned twenty, had been enrolled in secretarial college in Taipei, hadn't wanted to leave. She had friends there, a young life. Taipei at that time had 2 million residents; Niagara Falls, just under seventy thousand.

But Gong had seen places like the Canadian suburbs many times before and was more comfortable in this new terrain: He had trained as a pilot in Arizona and Colorado and spent time in New York and California for work. He had grown familiar with North American sprawl, with a vast uniformity unseen in the sheltered depth of the Taipei Basin. But I cannot erase my imagined memory of their shared longing for the warmth of Taiwan and its hills and the vision of a new land creeping up beneath them, the country ceaseless and cold.

My grandfather had been born into winter, in the rural lands beyond Beijing. Today's maps show me perfect, rectangular fields, a square of clustered buildings forming a dense village. The open homestead he wrote of in his letter is nowhere to be found. But I have formed its walls from his words and my mother's stories, inhabited the scene with this unknown family. Nearby sit our ancestors' tombs—unkempt, I imagine, for who is there to sweep the graves come springtime?

It was 1919, the Year of the Earth Sheep. The

Great War had not long ago finished, and the world was in the midst of negotiating what would become the Treaty of Versailles. In a small courtyard house in Hebei Province, my grandfather, Chung-chin, was the first boy in a family of sisters. He was nicknamed San-ni (Third Gentle Girl), as if a girl's name might make life easier.

The world outside grew turbulent. The aftershocks of Versailles rattled out in dispersion: The May Fourth protests had spawned a movement; student activists were proclaiming a new culture, seeking an end to the Confucianism that had shaped China for centuries. Nationalists, communists, and warlords allied and disavowed one another, purges and betrayals forming a brutal beat. The time was a blur to a young boy, coming into focus only when it touched Gong's small life: fleeing the conflicts and staying in far-off Beijing hutong houses in lanes with names like Bamboo Oblique Street, Pine Alley, Little Four Eyes Well. The March 18 Massacre in 1926—in which the military fired into a crowd of protestors, killing forty-seven—was a violent interlude he witnessed uncomprehendingly. Warlords and generals passed through town; their names he would recognize only in later life.

At home, Gong found some regularity and comfort. He slept each night in his grandmother's room and listened to stories each afternoon as he lay on his grandfather's tummy. From the age of five onward, he spent some of each day in the kitchen, learning to cook as he played sous chef to his mother. I imagine, now, that she taught him all the things that I remember, memories from my great-grandmother passed on as meals. Together they made fluffy mantou, packed into bamboo steamers in their small kitchen. They folded pork jiaozi and seared spiced Xinjiang lamb. In those early years, his mother taught him to cook an entire Chinese banquet, with formal dishes from every region. She died of heart failure in 1929, when my grandfather was ten.

"After that," he wrote in his letter, "it was as if the whole family scattered. In my memory, it was as if I was the only one who stayed in our old house in our old village."

I imagine him then, a quiet boy whose ties to home vanished the way steam runs into air.

Half the world away, in a different country, I watched Gong fold dumplings the way he had learned at his mother's hip seven decades earlier. He was nimble-fingered and gentle, and each dumpling was perfect on the plate. He shaped and laid out each folded bundle with care, offering them, perhaps, for inspection to a friendly, familiar ghost.

SHAN

n. MOUNTAIN; HILL

Mountains are shaped amid opposing forces: even as they are forced upward from the ground below, erosion wears them away.

5

AT FIVE IN THE MORNING, IN THE HAZE-BLUE period before light catches the mountains, I shuffle off the futon bed and onto the floor next to me. The others still sleep—their breaths catching every so often on their journeys toward waking—as I lace my boots and zip up my fleece, tracking my way silently to the door on rubber-soled tiptoes. The latch is dew-covered, and my hand slips as I press the door shut behind me.

The vale hangs heavy with clouds, and in that blue light, at the right angle, everything glistens. The deepest gash of the slopes is still shadowed, but in minutes the contours of the peaks grow haloed. Sun creeps into the morning around the eastern hillside and onto the terrace on which I stand, slightly chilled but warming at the thought of breakfast to come: coffee and steaming congee with salted turnip omelet.

I have joined a hiking group—ten strangers in all—brought together by a shared desire to escape the city, perhaps, or for the thinning air of high altitude. Some of them have come for Qilai Mountain's peak, logging its name among the others they've reached, and some have come simply to meet like-minded people, those enamored of the mountains. I've been drawn here by a sensory longing, a desire for exertion and cold breath in my lungs, for alpine scents.

In the gloaming hours of the night before, our van trundled too close to a cliff's edge after taking a wrong turn lower down in the valley. From where I stand now, I can see the road and the sheer chalky drop-off, a graying wound in the hillside. Beneath it is darkness, even as dawn works its way into day. I feel a twinge of relief, followed by a momentary shiver at the thought that it might have gone differently.

We set out toward the Nenggao trailhead after breakfast. The road follows a valley segmented by the Wanda Reservoir, a narrow turquoise strip held by the nearby Wushe Dam, construction of which began under the Japanese in the 1930s and was completed only in 1957, under the Nationalists. We pass the tip of the reservoir, known also as Bi Hu (Jade Lake), where sediment clouds the green. I stretch my gaze to the basin below, toward Lushan. The once-busy hot springs resort town has been all but abandoned, following a series of flash floods and mudslides that killed thousands in 2008 and 2009. Photographs of the disasters show buildings choked with the waste of the mountains, drawn downward by water. The mountains tipped multistory human constructions onto their sides. Driving past, I watch the surviving buildings sitting empty, gray as rockfall. Persistently, a handful of shops and hotels remain. The steep roads skirt the edge of a near-swallowed place.

Because of earthquakes and typhoons, the asphalt is in rough condition. The rutted lane was closed until a few days ago, as a small quake last week broke the road in half. With only one route up the mountain, the repairs were swift, shovelfuls of pitch and gravel spread into the gaps. But the road still has the split-open appearance of a loaf of bread.

·

IN THE EARLY QING DYNASTY, IN THE MID-seventeenth century, Taiwan and its mountains held little importance. The empire and its relationship to the world were understood in terms of five cardinal points—east, west, south, north, and center—with China, 中國 zhong guo ("middle country"), as the heart. Taiwan, by contrast, was viewed as a mere "ball of mud," well beyond the empire. Even once perceptions of the island changed—by necessity, because of its strategic positioning and wealth of resources—and though the plains and their indigenous communities were absorbed into the "civilizing" project of the empire, the regions beyond the mountains remained an unknowable wilderness.

Geologically, Taiwan's mountains seem precarious. Along the eastern coast, the peaks were formed by volcanic outflow, cooled lava and rock, and compacted ash fused by heat. In the Central Mountain Range, the bedrock is metamorphic; dappled and banded rock forms forged over time and under pressure from simpler stones. When seen in cross section, the vast movements that have made these mountains possible are clearly visible in parallel bands that run the axis of the land. The tectonic forces that pressed the island into being—from between the plates, beneath the sea—are evident to those who know what to look for. For geologists, Taiwan remains a new island, still in the throes of adolescent development. The mountain chains that first formed Taiwan are between just 6 and 9 million years old. In comparison, gneiss that formed 2,900 million years ago can be found in Scotland, and the volcanic ranges at Snowdonia can be dated to some 500 million years ago.

There is a pervasive tendency to ascribe mountains with permanence, but at the birth of modern geology, eighteenth-century uniformitarian geologists came up with the notion that mountains were changeable things, formed by the slow but perpetual flux of Earth's crust. They rejected the notion that the world was shaped quickly, through sudden catastrophic events, like biblical floods. Many resisted this new geology. Christian orthodoxy could make no room for a such a vast history of Earth itself. The mountains were the one thing in the landscape too vast to be moved, too sturdy to be toppled. In order to accommodate such an enormous scale of change, a wholly new perspective of time was needed: the world could not simply be six thousand years old but was surely much older, perhaps infinitely old. Geologists realized that given many millions of years the mountains, too, would wear away or disappear. The great peaks that had been thrust from seabeds would wither once more. That which had "seemed so durable, so eternal," as Robert Macfarlane writes in *Mountains of the Mind*, took on a "baffling mutability."

Two centuries later, I first ventured into Taiwan's Central Mountain Range. Behind the apparent solidity of these mountains, I would find fragility: landslides, earthquakes, erosion, rockfalls. Water, wind, and rain—the torrents of monsoons and typhoons—can carry more force than stone. With tectonic movement or a wet period, the island's slopes could be shaken to dust.

When I was twelve, a magnitude 5.4 quake rattled beneath my hometown in southern Ontario. The school term had begun a few weeks earlier, but the dregs of summer were with us still. A group of us had gathered on the lawn outside school, absentmindedly pulling blades of grass from the ground, squabbling over the lyrics to a pop song, when the trembling began. My knees shook as I sat cross-legged, and I thought I was having some kind of nervous reaction, so I pressed them down, not wanting the other girls to see. But when I looked up, they were all trembling too, ever so slightly, the way one might before an exam or a first date.

That small quake rattled a few dishes from their shelves but was largely imperceptible to those who weren't paying attention. My mother, driving across town to pick me up from school, didn't notice it at all, and if she had noticed, I cannot say she would have remembered it: small earthquakes were a regular occurrence in her childhood. But for me, born onto a comparatively stable landmass, every detail has remained.

In Taiwan, historical archives record only the most destructive of earthquakes. Before regular monitoring began at the end of the nineteenth century, written reports in government correspondence, diaries, and travel books recounted only those that destroyed towns, killed villagers, brought ocean to land, and rent great gaps in the ground. Prior to the rise of geology and seismology as scientific disciplines in the late nineteenth century, mild quakes were regular occurrences not worth remarking upon.

Modern geological study came to East Asia through a circuitous route. By the mid-nineteenth century, Western geology had roundly challenged the view that Earth was a short-lived, unchanging place, and uniformitarian geologists like Charles Lyell—who drew heavily on the work of the Scotsman James Hutton—had popularized the notion that the Earth's history could be understood as a slow process of wear, tear, and transformation. Chinese science and philosophy had for many centuries made maps and studies of its territory, conducted seismological studies, designed seismological instruments, and even classified minerals, fossils, and the development of landforms. As early as the Tang dynasty, it was conjectured that the fossils found on mountaintops had once lain far beneath the sea. But in early nineteenth-century China, there was little semblance of a geological science as the uniformitarians knew it.

The sixth edition of Lyell's *Elements of Geology*—a

field guide of sorts, intended to be paired with his earlier, theoretical *Principles of Geology*—was the first uniformitarian text to be translated into Chinese. In 1865, translators commissioned by Qing officials set to the ambitious task of interpreting a text with often untranslatable words—fossil names, "Miocene," "mammoth"—in what came to be titled *Dixueqianshi*. According to the scholar Mariko Takegami, the act of translation was a trial. The foreign interpreter and Chinese translator had a limited understanding of one another's languages, and it is said that the process gave the translator nightmares of ossified beasts.

But the work was considered vital to Qing dynasty China, which was keen to develop and make use of its natural resources, particularly through mining. The pursuit of geological knowledge became inextricably bound up with the prosperity and status of the land and its people. The first Chinese geologists were sent to study variously in Japan, Scotland, England, and Belgium. Likewise, American and German geologists conducted many of the first geological surveys in Chinese territory. Japan, too, engaged European scientists. The Chinese translation of *Dixueqianshi* became well known in Japanese scientific circles, where readers translated the geological terminology into Japanese, which then made its way back to China.

The geological sciences were thus shaped by a process of exchange among the West, China, and Japan.

The early development of seismology and its instruments benefited vastly from research carried out by British researchers working in Japan, which, like Taiwan, is located on the Ring of Fire. John Milne, widely considered to be a founding father of modern seismology, was an English mining engineer. In 1876, he took up a position as a professor of mining and geology in Tokyo and four years later helped found the Seismological Society of Japan. Alongside his fellow British researchers Alfred Ewing and Thomas Gray, Milne began research on seismological instruments, resulting in the development of modern pendulum seismometers.

When the First Sino-Japanese War resulted in Taiwan's transfer from Qing China to Japan on May 8, 1895, these new sciences became key to understanding the freshly acquired terrain. Two years later, the first Gray-Milne seismometer was installed in Taipei—renamed Taihoku by the Japanese—enabling the official collection of seismic data on the island. Just three years later, amid a much wider survey of the land and its people, Japan commissioned the first geological survey of Taiwan, *A Map of Geology and Mineral Resources of the Island of Taiwan*, using comparisons with the Japanese landscape to account for the island's lithic features. These early surveys are a window not just into the origins of geology in East Asia but also into the shifting cultural landscape of Taiwan during the Japanese period.

After two centuries of Chinese rule, the Taiwanese people—both indigenous and the many who had migrated from southern China since the seventeenth century—were subject to the linguistic and cultural dominance of a new empire. Japanese rule was marked by efforts to make official much of what had remained uncharted while Taiwan was regarded as a wild outpost of Chinese civilization. Along with the land surveys, a census was taken and economic studies were conducted. The Japanese sought to map and manage the entirety of the indigenous territories in the remote mountains. Taiwanese students were absorbed into the Japanese educational system, and infrastructure was modernized. Japanese maps were created to show sea routes between Taiwan and Japan, a means for threading the Japanese archipelagos and Taiwan together. A terrain that was once oriented toward the Taiwan Strait and the mainland beyond came to be understood in relation to a new motherland in the east.

Likewise, the arts were used to consolidate Japanese governance. In 1909, as Japanese administrators worked their way inland from the plains, Ishikawa Kinichiro, now considered one of the fathers of Taiwanese landscape painting, was sent to draw topological maps of the Central Mountain Range. According to the art historian Yen Chuan-yin, Ishikawa often sat under military guard, painting the forested slopes. The works Ishikawa produced were then sent on to Tokyo to demonstrate the colonial government's success in "civilizing" the wilder reaches of the "savage" island. These early visions of the Taiwanese landscape—a body of work which is said to have inspired much of the rural-focused art that came to characterize the island's painterly style—became forever linked to colonial efforts to open up and survey the remote mountains.

The development of Taiwanese visual arts in the early twentieth century led to the formalization of arts education—Ishikawa taught painting at the Taipei Normal School and was a mentor to many leading landscape painters of the period—and helped channel budding Taiwanese artists toward studying in Japan. The government sponsored art exhibitions focusing on Taiwanese landscape and organized surveys asking locals to rank the beauty of the island's scenic destinations. Climbing mountains was encouraged as a pastime alongside the arts.

Ishikawa's paintings of the island reflect the sentiments of the time: while his Japanese watercolors are rendered in delicate hues with Mount Fuji a soft analogue for all mountains, his Taiwanese paintings are more fully saturated and less formally composed; the hills and forests are crass and unsubtle. Bold greens and bright hues marked out in strong strokes characterize the island's heat and bounty. In his painting *The Second Highest Mountain in Taiwan*, Snow Mountain's peaks are a light-smeared white, the slopes a blotted marine blue. The trees are not delicate adornments, but immoderate, deep-hued shapes in the foreground. Images like Ishikawa's—in paintings, maps, and surveys—sought to position the island within the broader empire, to render the teeming island knowable.

•

MY EARS POP AS WE CLIMB HIGHER. THE SMALL van trundles along the gravel shoulder that serves as a parking lot. Vehicles cluster the side of the road; other hikers have made an earlier start. I step out, tighten my pack, and feel the chill of altitude prickle my skin. Clouds dapple the tips of the green mountain crests, and sun pours through the gaps. The morning will warm up. I tighten my laces and venture toward the narrow track.

The head of the Nenggao Cross-Ridge Trail is just east of Wushe. The town is marked by its history: In late October 1930, the Wushe Rebellion marked a last stand of indigenous resistance to colonial rule. A group of Seediq people, led by their chief, Mona Rudao, ambushed and killed more than 130 Japanese officials and families attending a sports day. They had seen decades of land enclosure, which followed the North American models of forcing indigenous communities onto reserves, as well as forced labor—camphor and cypress logging in traditional territories. This resulted in mounting daily tensions between Japanese police and villagers. In the weeks that followed, the government deployed some 2,000 troops and police officers to retaliate, alongside more than 1,000 rival indigenous people, playing local tribal hostilities to their favor. The Seediq took to the mountains, which they knew far better than the Japanese. The military then resorted to heavy artillery and aerial bombardment with gas bombs to quash the uprising, said to be the first use of chemical warfare in Asia. Decades later, the uprising would be propagandized by Chinese Nationalists seeking a tale of Taiwanese opposition to Japanese rule. But Wushe's history is a telling case of resistance amid centuries of erasure of the island's indigenous communities under both Japanese and Chinese regimes.

In the decades preceding the uprising, Japanese officials had made use of older indigenous trails to suppress local tribes and form a direct passage between the western and eastern sides of the island. The Nenggao Trail was used primarily by police and, following the turnover to the Chinese Nationalists after the Second World War, by Taiwan Power to route an east–west transmission line. Informational placards, an aging kiln used by Japanese police, and suspension bridges built by Taiwan Power remain now: the remnants of this fragmented past litter the mountainside.

But there are relics, too, of a longer territorial tale, told in the scarred stone, where boundless swathes of rock have been laid bare. Brittle slate, argillite, and phyllite, cleaved and folded together, make up these mountains. As steady as I imagine rock to be, the trail is a shattered reminder of its fragility.

In 2009, in the course of just a weekend, Typhoon Morakot brought more than 2,500 millimeters of rain to Taiwan, more than three times the United Kingdom's average yearly rainfall. The region around Nenngao was badly affected. Huge swathes of the mountains slipped down toward the Choshui River.

This slate belt in the Central Mountain Range is just one such region on an island plagued by landslides, susceptible to threats from ground and sky. Landslides take place through the force of gravity and the agency of water or wind. Earthquakes make the slopes more susceptible to rain's damage. In ranges where shale, slate, and schist predominate, landslides are always a possibility, triggered perhaps by the force of a single quake or the deluge of a powerful storm— or, in unlucky cases, both. Around Taiwan, where land has been cleared for plantations or mineral excavation, to say nothing of the worsened storms wrought by climate change, much of the risk is anthropogenic.

After the storm, researchers using satellite imagery estimated that the area had suffered more than a thousand landslides, their riverine streams of shale and slate visible on the maps. At home, before setting out, I looked through diagrams of mass wastings, through statistics on rainfall and emergency warning systems, and through geological studies of the island's worst slides. The mountain might slough its old skin off in a range of ways—as a large rockfall, as debris flow, as a single portion detached and deposited downhill. I pulled images of the area up on my computer screen, zooming in on the largest landslide, which looked like its very own range, mountains in miniature formed by the contours of splintered rock on its scarps. I could follow its course downhill, flowing into the vale as water from a torrent, joining in tributaries with other rockfalls on the descent. From the map's scale, I plotted its size: half a kilometer across, a pale scar reaching deep into the green depths below. The image—snatched from a satellite beyond the sky—had its drama. But in the face of the landslides on Nenggao, knowing their mechanics does little to allay my terror.

I am not especially afraid of heights: I dabbled in rock climbing as a teenager and took a genuine pleasure in scaling walls and small slopes. But I've grown clumsy as an adult, suffering occasional bouts of fainting or motion sickness. Confronting the first small landslide, I begin to doubt my own footing. I wonder if, perhaps, this will be the moment I forget entirely how to walk. A hard-packed line of grit traces the route across, compacted by the hikers ahead, but there is an unnerving height to the landslide, stretching as it does from the cliffside above to the treed reaches below. Until my legs prove themselves to be working normally, I press myself forward, focusing solely on another hiker's pack directly ahead of me. Only when I have expunged any irrational worry of sending myself over the edge with a nervous twitch or unwilled leap can I take in the view.

Rock-felled trees and the remains of a metal bridge sit broken below, surrounded by scree. I swallow my breath, troubled by the force of it, and keep walking. We pass a small land god shrine—common in these mountains for those who wish to pay their respects—and then reach the first outpost, the Yunhai power station, where the group pauses for a snack, relieved for a moment of our weighty packs. I've overpacked and am already tired. But time runs short here. I force a cluster of dried mangos and nuts down and take a small swig of water before shouldering my pack for the afternoon.

The largest landslide sits a short distance away, and we approach it in single file. The green trees open to a mass of gunmetal and heather gray slipping into the distances below and above. On the satellite image, I was able to confine the space of the landslide between my thumb and index finger. My understanding of its magnitude on the screen was clipped, intellectual, and cold. The first slide was navigable because it was short. The second stretches half a kilometer ahead of me, exposed to air and height and little else. A moonwalk, perhaps, or a scorched battlefield might come close.

I take my first steps on the landslide, which slopes downhill into the packed mounds of gravel that form the mountain wall. Every movement exudes a smell of dust and heat, a sensation magnified by the chomp of my boots on the brittle ground. The path winds into a clavicle of the mountain, emerging on the other side in a great, lumbering swerve that leads around a bend and disappears. DO NOT LINGER, a sign at the landslide's edge states in bold letters.

I quicken my pace and attempt to take in the wasteland's enormity. It stretches to a height farther than I can fully see, a crisp line of gray forming a dark edge against the sky. The trees on either side are a hard seam of shadowed life, abruptly ending at the mineral border. Below the trail, slate, banded metamorphosed schists, and quartz sit tumbled together, a geologic record spilled over by the force of gravity. I keep moving. Sunlight glints off the occasional crystalline stone, giving the slope a fine sparkle, faint enough to miss in the lava-dark overflow. As if by instinct, my eye seeks out the sprouts of green that have sprung up in patches, returning vegetal life to the world of stone.

Pines are among the first trees to restore landslide areas in these mountains, stretching their roots to knit strength back into the earth. Reforestation projects now seek to speed up this work of nature. Where soil has eroded and typhoon winds and monsoon rains have degraded a slope, regeneration can be difficult. But where seedlings take hold and "tree islands" grow up, the slopes fare better. The trees draw moisture to the soil, and heavy winds are slowed by their crowns. The groves attract birds seeking shelter, who in turn sow the seeds of further growth. Unseen beneath the ground, the work of root systems begins to stabilize the soil structure. So when the forests disappear from the slopes, the mountains, too, are not long for this world. Landslides tell us how little is eternal.

6

I CANNOT ACCOUNT FOR WHY PO HID THE LET-
ter or kept us from the family with which she was so
clearly in contact. But it was not the first of such puz-
zles: She had grown erratic in old age. In the decade
after my grandfather's death, my mother and I often
visited her, and I would sip tea while trying to follow
their conversation in Mandarin. I learned the words
for criticisms, for complaints, and the expression my
mother's face took on when she held her tongue. I
thought often about something my grandmother
had said to me in passing—"The lashings I gave your
mother weren't half of what my mother gave me"—
and wondered how we'd managed her behavior for so
long, shrugging it off as a quirk of personality.

Years ago, just before I was due to move to
Germany, we had taken her to lunch at a sushi place

she enjoyed, and things were strained. She turned abruptly from praising me to criticizing my mother, spitting her words between mouthfuls. She was perpetually angry that my mother thought she needed more care. She permitted no one to help.

When we returned to her apartment, her anger shifted to something less defined, uneasy and uncontrollable. She hugged me a little too tight for a little too long, and I sensed the shift as it welled up through her body.

Po fell to the ground weeping and clutched my hands tighter than I had imagined a ninety-year-old woman could. She screamed in Mandarin and then in English: "If you go, I don't want to live anymore. I'll never see you again." She made for the balcony, moving quickly. I lurched forward and held her back, trying not to injure her brittle limbs as they flailed. Her wrists had grown so thin. How was she this strong?

I looked to my mother to call for help while Po clutched at my ankles, toppling us both, and made for the balcony once more. I tried to hold her still, to reason with her. "I will come back. I will see you again."

But I thought of my grandfather, how I hadn't seen him go.

An ambulance came, and the paramedics removed her grip, the fingers wound around me like roots. She ran toward the balcony again, and they restrained her. A needle, and she was quiet.

When we arrived at the hospital she smiled placidly from the gurney. I felt unsure of what we had done and regretted bringing her there. I wondered if I had overreacted. The geriatric specialist came and then the psychologist. They told us there was nothing wrong: she did not have dementia; she was not a risk to herself. She had in fact been particularly friendly to all the doctors. Would we like to see a social worker?

I felt rattled, fury and pity and grief intermingled, and did not know how to approach Po. She had leaped toward death, and I had held her back. I remembered a story she had told me one afternoon over a decade earlier.

In 1929, in Nanjing, China, my grandmother died. She was five years old. At nine in the morning, her heartbeat had stopped. No one was alarmed; she had been prone to fainting spells and often enacted a range of amateur dramatics that frustrated both her mother and the servants of the house. But when she didn't begin to move within a few minutes, the family panicked.

Feebly, they attempted to revive her, pinching her arms and lighting incense. They massaged her chest, rubbed her feet (her third toe marked with the birthmark I share). Exasperated, they applied warm cloths, but nothing worked. By evening, they gave up. Her father ordered that a door be removed from its hinges and placed on the floor. They laid her young body on its back, ready to be buried.

One of the kitchen hands intervened.

"Noble madam, have you given up reviving Kwei-lin so soon?" he asked.

"We don't know what else to do," her mother replied, breaking her silence.

"You didn't even take her to the hospital. You didn't call for a doctor!" the young man cried. "If you don't want to be bothered, please let me assume responsibility."

With permission from the family, the kitchen hand ran into town just before sunset. He returned accompanied by an old junk collector, known also to locals as an acupuncturist. The family, having resigned themselves to their daughter's death, allowed the old man to do as he saw fit. Squatting to the ground, he assessed the situation. He reached into his bag and unpacked a wooden box holding an array of needles. Silently, with precision, he inserted gold needles in rows of two from the top of her head down to her narrow heels. At pressure points he added a further ten pairs of needles, until her body resembled a glittering, doll-like pincushion. Satisfied, he settled in his crouched position and told the family to wait.

They waited three hours, shuffling around the house quietly. At eleven o'clock that night, a rasping sound came from Kwei-lin's throat. Quite suddenly, she sat upright—the gold needles glinting in the lamplight—and screamed.

"Ma!" Mother.

Returned from the dead, seemingly intact and with all her limbs working normally, my grandmother resumed her life. Though she always fretted about her weak heart, having seen what lay on the other side of the living, she never fainted again.

•

BEYOND THE LANDSLIDES, WHERE CLOUDS tumble at the fringes of the Nenggao Trail, the moss-damp forest grows thick. It progresses from the oaks and cypresses of the lower elevations to the perfumed air of hemlock and fir, banding in rings of forest around the slopes with our ascent. Every species has a stretched-out quality, carpeting one another, reaching toward the thin light. Lichen glows from the exposed rock walls, blanketing the mountain with a bryo-phyte gleam, resting in shadow, awaiting rain. The mosses drape and hang on the trees, too, shielding the Formosan flamecrests that perch on the branches. As I walk farther, white pines begin to reach over the mountain's outcrops into the nothingness of sky, moving toward the veil of pale clouds that gathers in the valley between here and the peaks of Nenggao Mountain, an ink-dark interruption on the bright horizon.

Hiking groups divide along natural rhythms, the peak-baggers racing ahead, hiking poles swinging with the regularity of their gait. I inevitably loll behind, far more interested in the minutiae of the ground than the goal of a distant crag. The trail cuts over reptilian ridges toward the sheltered side of Qilai Mountain, and I savor my slow pace. A fellow hiker— keen also to take time for photographs and the small glimpses only possible when one gets down on the ground to see a species at eye level—falls into step beside me.

Christoph is from Munich, and though I haven't felt myself missing my home in Germany, I am excited to salt our conversation with German words, feeling their elongated shape in the back of my mouth, unlike Mandarin, which occupies my teeth and lips. We chatter through the afternoon, bringing thoughts of literature and landscape poetry to the side of the mountain. He tells me of Kafka's story "The Great Wall of China"—a story of empire, national identity, and the eponymous wall's construction—and of Taiwanese painters he has grown to love. A dramaturgy professor who spends every spare minute in the mountains, he is nearing the end of a lengthy sabbatical in Taipei. The mountains have a hold on him, and he seems dejected about leaving.

It is mid-conversation on an exposed stretch of trail when we both abruptly stop: a pocket of air smells of almonds and fresh-baked cakes, sweet and sugared. We instinctively look upward to a nearby flowering tree and press our noses to it with disappointment. It smells of nothing, and we realize that with one step forward and one step back the perfume disappears. I look at the side of the trail but there is little but packed soil. Frustrated, I turn to the ditch near the precipice and see a scattered range of herbs and shrubs, one patch of red-green leaves starred with tiny white inflorescences. We tuck ourselves low to the ground—Christoph crouching from a towering Teutonic height—and the scent intensifies, an extraordinary wonder from such minuscule flowers. We each take a photograph, wondering what the plant might be, but it will take weeks before I track it down and match the scent to its flower: *Persicaria chinensis,* also called creeping smartweed or Chinese knotweed.

Its tiny blooms have the look of rice—indeed, in Taiwan, one of its common names is rice smartweed—scattered amid the green carpet of the trailside. Native to Taiwan and southeast Asia, it tends toward ditches near villages and the slopes of tea farms in the lower hills. When it has sought foreign shores, the vine has been labeled invasive. But here, in the upper reaches of its home range, it is a thing of beauty. Sweetened by its breath, I am carried upward toward the tree line.

•

IN 1900, BUNZO HAYATA ARRIVED IN TAIWAN for a two-month sojourn before beginning his studies in Tokyo. It was the culmination of more than ten years of longing to formally study botany: the twenty-six-year-old Hayata had been long waylaid in his efforts to complete his studies. Despite a keen interest as a teenager and his joining the Botanical Society of Tokyo, family obligations had delayed his entry into university.

By the time he embarked on graduate studies, his intellectual path had been marked out for him: his supervisor, Jinzo Matsumura, a pioneer in Taiwanese botany, decided that Hayata should focus not on mosses, as he desired, but on the flora of Taiwan. Hayata took to the topic wildly and with great ambition. With almost youthful zeal he sought to distinguish the flora of Taiwan from other regions in East Asia, noting that the conditions that had previously made it difficult to survey—the western flatlands unfolding to steep, inaccessible mountains that dropped to the eastern seacoast, and ranging from subtropical to alpine habitats—were precisely what made it unique. Once the Japanese government worked its way into the higher mountain ranges, as it had along the Nenggao Trail, new pathways opened for botanical expeditions. In 1911, after several years of study both in Japan and Taiwan, followed by a period visiting herbaria in London (at Kew Gardens), Berlin (at Dahlem), Paris, and St. Petersburg, he published the first volume of his *Icones Plantarum Formosanarum*. In its opening pages, Hayata outlined an ambitious, multivolume plan: "For a long time, I have had a desire to publish a flora of Formosa . . . which might be completed in fifteen years." In reality, he devoted ten years and as many botanical excursions to producing a ten-volume flora, cataloguing 3,658 species and 79 varieties across nearly 1,200 genera and 170 families of vascular plants.

Hayata's legacy remains in the names of plants today: botanist Hiroyoshi Ohashi has counted more than 1,600 Taiwanese plant names listing Hayata as their author among the more than 2,700 species named by him in his excursions across East and Southeast Asia. But his ability to catalogue so wide a range of flora was partly because his work coincided with Japanese incursions into previously inaccessible territory. Botanists in the previous century had simply been unable to reach those places.

Of course, many of the island's plants were known and named by those who lived there. But efforts to document, catalogue, and distinguish Taiwanese species from others worldwide began in earnest with the rise and spread of modern taxonomy, which itself had developed but a century earlier. As with geology, Western botanical sciences came to the island through exploration and colonial expansion. In 1853, the Scottish botanist Robert Fortune—most famous for his theft of Chinese tea plants and processing methods in order to establish British tea production in India—catalogued a number of coastal plants, marking the first record of botanical study on the island. In the 1860s, Robert Swinhoe, an English biologist who was also a consul in Taiwan, surveyed the island's natural history, and in the late nineteenth century, the Irish botanist Augustine Henry published a list of nearly 1,500 Taiwanese plant species.

Scientific labels contain so much of the past, entire histories rendered in nomenclature: the many plant and animal species named for Swinhoe, like *Lophura swinhoii* (Swinhoe's pheasant); or *Fagus hayatae* (Taiwan beech) and the genera *Hayatella* (a Rubiaceae genus endemic to Taiwan, recorded just once, on the east of the island) named for Hayata. Yushan (Jade Mountain), Taiwan's highest peak, was for many years known as Mount Morrison, named for a foreign sea captain. More than a hundred species are named for the mountain, many of them recorded by Hayata himself. Morrison's name thus remains in the botanical record: from *Berberis morrisonensis* (Taiwan barberry) to *Angelica morrisonicola*.

Language is a tricky thing: scientific labels cannot delimit the many names by which our world is ordered. As I learned the plants in Taiwan, I learned to match their common names to their scientific binomials, Mandarin names to Taiwanese. Once in a while, I found no English translation, and a plant was left to exist only in the linguistic limits of my mind; I could name but a tiny fraction of this island, and much remained caught between worlds. I began to write them out, using the gridded worksheets given to me by a Mandarin teacher in Berlin, noting the names of plants in English, in traditional characters, and transliterating their pronunciation for myself in Pinyin. 八角金盤 was bajiao jinpan—"octagonal gold plate" fatsia. 鞭打繡球 was bianda xiuqiu, a forb with no common name in English but whose Chinese name means "whip hydrangea." I wrote them out in Latin, as if it rendered the names stable: *Fatsia polycarpa*, *Hemiphragma heterophyllum*.

But between languages, words are unsteady: when I asked my mother to name plants or places, she often wrote out their names in Wade-Giles romanization, a transliteration of Mandarin used around the world until the 1980s when Hanyu Pinyin from mainland China became the common standard. My mother read the translation of my grandfather's letter and came back confused, struggling to match places she knew with their new transliterations. In text messages, I used Pinyin names and places, and my mother would reply frustrated that she couldn't understand them. Pinyin was a new-fangled, mainland thing; how could q be pronounced "ch," or x as "hs," she asked. It didn't make any sense, she concluded.

I didn't need to tell her how much had changed. A gap opened between us every time we put our words into writing.

•

A STORM HAS BEEN BATTERING THE TENT ALL night. I can feel it seeping through the fly sheet, the luminous cold of mountain rain penetrating the walls. At 2:30 in the morning, the mountain is inked in darkness. But I cannot put off getting up any longer. I delicately try, without touching the walls of the soaked tent, to dress. Leggings, rain pants, dry socks. I work a shirt, fleece, and jacket over my shoulders, pulling the hood down tight. I unzip the tent and flick on my headlight.

Torrents of water howl past, and I suppress an urge to return to the warmth of my sleeping bag. Before setting out on the hike, while researching the landslides, I read up on the mountain nicknamed Black Qilai, and came across a chronological list of hikers who had died on its more treacherous northern slopes. I put this out of my mind now, shaking as I struggle to tie my boots. From the Nenggao Trail, the route over the mountain will be much safer, a kilometer of steps followed by an alpine track and a brief scramble to the south peak. But if Qilai is tormented by ghosts, as the rumors go, then the storm seems to call them forth.

The sky roils with dark clouds and is blacker still

for the emptiness of the new moon as we make for the peak, hoping to arrive for sunrise. With my headlight lit, I can just about see the wind that tangles persistently around the other members of the group. Rain streaks across my field of vision. The only relief is in the low shelter of the grassy Yushan cane lining the stone path. The steps are oil-slick and running with mud. I look down, narrowing my attention to every movement I make, listening for a rhythm in the click of my hiking stick and the rustle of the grass in the wind. Beyond the krummholz, the crooked wood of high mountain ranges known in Chinese as 高山矮曲林 gao shan ai qu lin (or "high mountain low-bent forest"), we pass the final stands of cane on the tree line, the green wall around us quickly shrinking.

At the top of the steps, a meadowland flashes into view. Despite the work of the climb, I am chilled with a skeletal, creaky sort of cold. I think back to yesterday morning, my longing to breathe thinner air, the scent of the smartweed. I am guilty of idealizing the trip, imagining a view and a sense of intimacy with the mountain. Instead, I feel alienated by it; I can hardly see, and what I can see is sodden.

Halfway across the meadow, a large group of hikers has stalled, their matching rain ponchos stretched over their packs so they look not unlike a caterpillar.

The trail ahead has turned to swamp, and they've stepped into the scrub in hopes of avoiding it. Making little progress, they pick their way through the plants, humpbacked and achingly slow. I look to my own group, ready to step into the scrub myself, when I see the others plow forward along the soaked trail. Their expressions require no explanation. There can be no more complaint, no more room for pause. I follow, sinking to my ankles, feeling water seep through every hole in my battered boots. We are nearing the peak, and the conditions are too brutal for discussion. I tuck my chin inside my jacket, breathing warmth into my neck, a small solace.

We reach plateaus of smaller plants, growing minutely and staunchly in the cold. The ground is a tangle of evergreen shrubs that are dull without their summer flowers, short-cropped rushes, prickling meadow plants, and the puckered leaves of stonecrop sedum clustering at this height. It looks like a Scottish moor transported across the world. Most of the plant names remain unknown to me in the darkness. With time, I know these plants will recede even farther from reach: both climate change and increased use of the mountains are pushing lower-elevation species to higher altitudes. Warmth ascends the peaks like islands in a montane sea, and the alpine plants have nowhere to go but up. Through the predawn storm I watch the ground in passing, the plants grown from wind and stone, seeking the coldest part of a warm island.

At the base of the peak, the plants dwindle, and only long-lived rocks stand ahead. Wind pummels my jacket, pressing it tight against my frame. I press on, reaching my hands out to pull myself up meter-high stones, planting my hiking stick in the mud below me. With every jab and release I see rainwater pooling in the holes I've left. With little else to occupy my mind, I begin to count steps. One, jab, two, jab, three, jab, ever upward. Sweat drips a trail down my chest and back, mingling with the rainwater. I begin to feel sensations in isolation: the tunneled sound of the wind against my hood, my pulse hot in my ears, the tastes of salt and chalk in my mouth. I feel myself dissolve in movement the way sediment flows downriver.

I am roused from the labored trance of climbing to find an open windswept meadow at Qilai's south peak. Rocks are scattered around the perimeter of this high point where a chipped yellow aluminum sign hangs from a chain welded to a boulder. 3358 M, it reads.

I thought, when I first heard of it, that the mountain was named Qi for 七 ("seven"), but its name 奇萊山 pleases me more. 奇 qi means "to be astonished, surprised," and 萊 lai (like the second character in Penglai, the mythic island) means either "lamb's quarters" or, as I prefer to imagine, the more archaic "meadow." It brings to mind the plants here, their cold peaks disappearing like islands beneath a swallowing sea.

We take turns in the darkness, posing in the glare of one another's headlights to snap photographs of each of us holding the battered sign. It is icy to touch, but in exhaustion I care little. I wanted the light of the sky, to sense something of height and stone, and what I got was a deluge. I wanted a view, perhaps, a feeling of having the range unfolded beneath me like a map, but the mountains refused to show themselves. But I do not feel disappointment. I grin for my photograph, air gusting into my lungs, and in that cold shock, endorphins force their way through my body. I suddenly feel the elation of movement.

The sun rises without our noticing, muffled behind the gray of the clearing storm as we descend. The waxing light is dull, with mist softening the edges of Qilai's crags and cliffs. Despite it all, I begin to feel warm. Like the flicker of lamplight evacuating the night, I feel a small glow in having seen the storm.

THE CHLORINE HAZE HUNG LOW TO THE ground. The mist, resisting the gravity of the fall, had carried it upward. I leaned over the railing, catching a glimpse of the roiling white, and then ducked back, shaking. I'd been to Niagara so many times, but still the waterfall scared me.

It couldn't have smelled that way, I'm sure. It's a trick of my mind, adding detail to scenes I've not been in for decades. Unable to pin down the ionic scent of fast-moving water, I've substituted the smell of swimming pools. The fountains nearby, where Po used to take us to watch the water dancing, backlit in blue and pink: *they* smelled of chlorine. We'd been there every summer, on the weekends when Po and Gong ventured with us into town from their bungalow on Armstrong Drive.

Those moments I remember with clarity. The plush blue velvet seats of the Oldsmobile, the crumbs of some long-finished snack worked down into the seams. Stacks of McDonald's napkins were stuffed into the center console, and a discarded coffee cup—stained and milk-sticky—lay crumpled on the floor. The plastic cassette tapes clicked as they unspooled to play Chinese ballads. And all the way, Gong sat smiling in the back seat, gripping the safety handle on the ceiling of the sedan. It never made much sense to me as a child: I knew he'd flown fighters and imagined him tracing loop-the-loops in the sky, rolling upside down like the jets we saw at the air show each spring. But he never drove the car.

I wonder now when his mind began to change. Had it already started when I was ten, when he came to stay for a weekend and cooked my favorite tea eggs? At thirteen, I saw him rest in complete darkness on his bed—a wooden plank laid atop a soft mattress, as he'd slept in his military training—and just lay there, silent. I couldn't stay still as a child, so I couldn't understand it. Something had to have been wrong. Had he changed by then?

The small, incremental shifts in the brain begin years before we can notice them.

When he'd begun writing the letter, his memory was already failing. Detail remained, but order had gone.

Still, his details were sharp.

IN JULY 1937, THE SECOND SINO-JAPANESE WAR began. A Japanese soldier failed to return to his post after a military exercise in Chinese territory in Beijing. When Japanese forces were refused entry to the Wanping fortress to find him, tensions rose, and there were the first flares of all-out war. Much of this history hangs on mishap: it is said the soldier returned to his post later that evening, having merely been lost. But forces clashed outside the fortress that night, along a bridge of carved granite, where water flowed heavy in the Yongding River. The beginning of the war thus became known as the Marco Polo Bridge Incident. My grandfather had just come of age in his small northern village.

He had hardened himself to the coming war. As a teenager, he'd gone to study military management, shaving his head and purging himself of the softness of the years he'd spent curled up with his nainai, from the afternoons following his mother through the kitchen. He slept on wooden planks—a habit I realize he never shook—and began bathing in ice water. With the war begun, he escaped to find his father, who'd left and remarried, only to be turned away and sent back on the same train.

Millions of people moved west, outrunning the advancing Japanese army. Soldiers dismantled the railway tracks as they traveled, hoping to stem the pursuit. Alone, at eighteen, my grandfather took the road west in a cobbled-together journey of buses and cars, traveling some twelve hundred miles across China. He was lucky; most people went on foot.

In meetings and in partings, serendipitous forces draw some together and others apart. On the road, my grandfather met an old school friend he'd not seen in years, Liu Shen, who encouraged him to stop at Guiyang to finish high school and prepare for university entrance examinations. My grandfather wished to study architecture or engineering, wanting a quiet job in which he could apply focus and precision, but that was not to be. One connection led to the next. They coincided with recruitment for the Republic of China Air Force. Liu Shen recognized the examining officer as a classmate of his brother's. And so both he and my grandfather took their first steps in the air force.

7

THE MORE MONTHS I SPENT IN TAIWAN, THE easier it was to forget the world outside. The years I'd spent in Britain, chasing a paternal past, grew hazy. I spoke with what childlike Mandarin I could and grew unashamed of it. It got better. My limbs acquainted themselves with warmth. In Taipei, I traced my route on the MRT lines without thought, winding through alleys I'd learned every inch of. I began to learn the trails, where tree-darkened tracks would lead to sheltered peaks, and took to them regularly.

Then, a setback: a woman approached me on a bus, pressed her thumb and forefinger around my cheeks. Hen piaoliang ("very pretty"). A Westerner, she concluded. I chafed in reply. My cheeks burned.

A taxi driver asked me why my Mandarin was so good for a foreigner. "My mother is from Taiwan," I explained, and he turned on me in reprimand. "Then why is your Mandarin so poor?"

I retreated to the forests, but even there, once in a while, I felt unmoored. Thoughts of my grandparents came often as I walked the mountains, rhythm giving way to notions I dared not entertain in normal life. My stride worked itself into a charm, hypnotic, and the worst came to me. I hadn't done enough. Hadn't learned enough Mandarin, knew no Taiwanese at all, and hadn't taken enough of an interest. We had been too foreign for my grandmother, too Western. Had Po kept things from us on purpose? Had we done something to deserve it?

I composed her life in scenes, examining the fragments she had told me for long enough that they grew vivid, until I could no longer remember how much she had said and how much I'd added myself. I searched for evidence that she had mentioned our family, but my thoughts always came out misshapen: she had hidden things on purpose. I remained angry at how she had treated Gong, but this was displaced by my own guilt at not having done more. She had lost so much. I couldn't account for it.

Ten years ago, she let me commit her words to tape. We sat and recorded for an afternoon. Perhaps she hoped I might one day search them for meaning. She told me what she could stand to remember. My mother sat close by to translate. What my grandmother described was the world she had lost: the daughter of a wealthy Nanjing landowner and merchant, she'd believed her future was bright. She could not have imagined the scene in which she'd spend the last years of her life huddled in a dark, foreign home, barely pecking at bland reheated meals. But the details she told me only ever circled the stories: she spoke of fabrics, of commodities, of teahouses, and the minute details in the scenes but never of their players, never their places. In the years after I recorded her, I searched for that past world in books, fitting her stories into their timelines, hoping to grasp some of it from the distance of decades.

She named her family's businesses, counting them on the lank fingers of one hand.

1. A money lender
2. A grain wholesaler
3. A chandlery
4. A soybean processor
5. A bakery
6. A teahouse

They'd stood around a city block, a small empire into which she had been born. She was particularly fond of visiting the soybean factory, where she'd peer into porcelain jars of beans so large it took three men to lift them. The floor of the factory held hundreds of jars topped with woven lids, all filled and waiting to become soy sauce. Drawn by her sweet tooth, she had pilfered cookies and cakes from the bakery. The chandlery sold candles for every occasion—again, she counted these out on her aging digits—from plain ones for everyday use to red ones for festivals.

Life had its rhythms. Nanjing in the 1930s remained as ordinary as it could be in the midst of the civil war between the Nationalists and the Communists. My grandmother and her siblings devoted their days to study, and Po was skilled in languages and sums. She learned English, Cantonese, Japanese. In her spare time, she sewed, as if the gold needles that had once revived her had also imprinted their deft skill upon her hands. Sewing was the constant she carried with her. She sewed her way into later life, until cataracts clouded her vision, making me blankets and night-gowns, handing me down the clothes she'd sewn for my mother decades earlier.

She remembered textiles, always, and the scissors she used to clip images from fashion magazines, saving new designs for dresses. With good fabric and a small sewing machine at her disposal, she'd had no need for a tailor, designing every qipao she desired, adjusting the heights and cuts of the necklines, the puffs of the shoulders. The waistlines slimmed, and her palette grew bolder. She remembered one dress in particular, shaped in a light satin that flickered as she moved: it was flame orange.

My grandmother grew from girlhood to adolescence in the safety of that single city block. When the Japanese soldiers arrived in December 1937, it was from there that her family would flee.

•

AT SHUISHE MOUNTAIN SOME DAYS AFTER Nenggao, I count out the rutted and algal steps as I climb alone. The steps are the singular thing I can identify, a focus to train my thoughts on as the forest accumulates around me. The trail is a mesh of green, overgrown and rarely used, beginning south of Sun Moon Lake in central Taiwan. When I glanced at the surrounding hills from the distance of the lakeshore, the green formed a wall. Now I am well within it, the growth has thickened and surrounded me. I have a sense of what I might look for in the canopy: for ring-cupped oaks, chinquapins, camphor laurels, and beeches. But fern and taro overlap the path, branches hang heavy with lianas I do not know. I cannot see beyond the understory, which has wound its way over the top of the trail, forming a green tunnel that rises rapidly uphill. I struggle to bring order to the scene.

Learning a species is a way of quieting my thoughts. I do not have a good memory by nature: names slip away, as do faces; it is only when I take the time to draw a plant, to render its name in ink, that I stand a chance of knowing it. When I find a new plant, I write its name out repeatedly at home, tracing the lines of its leaves on the page. I do the same with hanzi, copying Chinese characters despite my clumsy script.

I cannot begin to know this place. I can hardly see my way to the next stretch of trail. The maps and surveys to which I usually turn are of little use here; nothing holds the growth at bay. I keep to the trail, buried beneath leaf mold, and duck beneath the spiderwebs strung between saplings and vines. The trail cants upward near-vertically in places.

I press on, legs quaking, steadying myself on branches. What was comfortable heat feels thickened beneath the wet canopy. My temper swells. A single fly pursues me, screaming into the air, as if it expects me to die at any moment among the ferns, and I melodramatically think for a second that indeed

I will die. I should never have attempted the trail on my own. This is not a place I could simply learn, and it is not mine anyway. I belong in a forest in a much bigger, colder country. I am not built for heat any more than my mother was built for winter. I speak in broken tones, making half sense to everyone I meet in Taiwan. My worlds exist in halves.

The forest closes around me. And it feels intentional.

Everything in my education had inoculated me against this kind of anthropocentrism: to resist the idea of nature as for us alone, of a forest providing arboreal answers to very human predicaments. But still I find myself falling short, seeing in this mountain a mirror for my misunderstandings, as if in knowing its nature I might find a way to belong to this place. I hoped for a breadcrumb trail through the winding wood. Breathless, I still harbor a longing that I might emerge into a clearing, with an empty sky and a clear-eyed moon, out beyond the forest line. To some understanding.

I climb onward until, half in tears at the crest of the slope, I emerge. The green glade stands serene, tucked onto a plateau halfway along the trail. The glade holds silence in its form—its occupants are tall and flexible in the wind, less suited to birds. Not trees but grasses, the culms are enormous and well spaced, so I traverse the gaps between them as an insect might a meadow. The green stalks rise to thrice my height, letting in shafts of olivine light that flicker in the movement of the leaves. The glade is silent, but vast: bamboo multiplies at a pace. Spreading rhizomatically, laterally, beneath the ground, they distract with their dizzying height, but the forest strides ceaseless across the ground, adding ever new culms to its ranks. The bamboo is cultivated here, spread in all directions. Stacks of felled culms lie off the side of the trail, and I wonder how anyone could make it up this brutal slope to retrieve them.

Months ago, my Mandarin teacher ran her pen down a page, marking out the skinny lines with six strokes: 竹 zhu ("bamboo"). She numbered each line, signposting their order for my future use, while repeating the stroke names under her breath: pie, heng, shu, pie, heng, shu gou. I mirrored her on my own page, repeating the tall-growing culms of the character in my notebook. And as they multiplied, a copse formed on the paper.

Now I press my lips to a pout and form the word 竹, my chin lifting with the rising tone. It comes out wrong. I try again, repeating the sound until I get the tone right, until I am breathless with the walk, and my frustration lifts.

Near the end of the glade, a small platform opens onto a vista. I can see already how far I've climbed. The steps wind their way up from the lake basin, swallowing a good deal of the altitude of the trek early on. From the platform, a stratum of thin clouds forms a visible seam between water and sky, the gray-white of their moisture hanging beneath the peaks opposite. From here, the entirety of Sun Moon's glacial blue shore is visible; its sunken curves surround the spit of forest reaching into it.

Rain begins to fall in small patters, so I press on to where a ridge rises up from the green. Water calls mosses under the rocky ledges to life, limning half-buried tree roots and rocks with a glistening sheen. Frayed ropes line the route, so I haul myself up their lengths, caked in the red-gold soil of the climb. In motion, little else but staying upright, moving onward, seems to matter. My breath heaves as I cover hundreds of meters of incline. And then, encircled by bundles of hikers' ribbons wrapped around trees—a woodland shrine to the mountain—I find the peak. The forest is erratic here, hacked and strewn with boulders. The peak is hardly a clearing in the trees. I circle the altitude marker, eyeing the trail from which I've come, and, disappointed, begin my descent.

I lumber down the ledges of tree roots, pressing my

hands to the trunks that line the path. The smooth bark at every difficult step shows the way; the well-worn handprints of hikers before me serve as trail markers for the descent. By the time I reach the bamboo again, the prints are shining glossy and green.

The forest offers no succor. Exhausted, with an aching left knee, I stumble through the flatter section of trail. There is a shuffle of leaves to my right, and a low, rattling grunt from between the culms. My pulse races as I search for the source of the sound. It rumbles again, higher in the canopy. The putty-brown form of a single male macaque—the size of a small child—slings its way between the bamboos, watching me as it moves. It glares, a fleshy, anthropomorphic face in the green, and approaches, still grunting. Macaques are territorial animals, and the call is unmistakably aggressive. I freeze, unsure of what to do beyond standing stock-still, stretching my shoulders to make myself appear as broad and tall as I can, backing away as if it is a bear. And as I do, he stops, watching the minutiae of my movements, locking with my gaze. In a few steps I am safe to turn on my heel and run. I do not look back.

My knee pulses in pain, and tears well up. What exactly was I hoping to find? Whatever I feel is inarticulate and excessive. I cannot encircle the forest with learned words and then claim to understand it. I want to know this place, to feel some sense of familiarity, but that is not simple, not an easy thing. I limp back to the town, watching the sky above the lake clearing from gray to blue. The mountain remains encased in cloud, indifferent to my movements across its heavy spine.

·

I STUDIED WEATHER REPORTS, MILITARY HIStories, and journals. I built myself a picture and inflected it with inherited words. The aerial bombardments over eastern had China persisted for months, bass notes in an aria of sirens. The bombs dropped on Nanjing exploded into the sun of the southern city through 1937's late-summer heat and continued into the darkening rain of autumn.

It had been high summer when the incident at Marco Polo Bridge occurred—the trigger of full-scale war—and my grandmother had spent July in the usual way, stretching her time between studying, sewing, and visits to the family stores. The distance to Beijing, to the war six hundred miles to the north, seemed incalculable.

But war arrived nonetheless. November swelled

in a torrent of rain, and as the cold set in toward December the family began preparations to depart. They would travel on foot, like most people, taking only what essentials they could down the choked and muddy routes westward. They escaped to Anhui, to my great-grandmother's family, who were rural landowners. My grandmother, just thirteen years old, had been fixated on growing up to become a modern woman. The brutality of war would, in a matter of days, make such a simple idea incomprehensible.

There were gaps in what Po told me, perhaps the things she never wished to speak about or things she'd merely forgotten in the telling. Links that connected the days of war that surely shaped her teenage years and might have explained so much of her to me. The war with Japan spanned her teens—forcing its way into her life and receding only when she turned twenty. Then, the confusion of the civil war returned. What might she have been like had things been different?

The remainder she told me in scraps. The family fled, but I don't know how long for. She never spoke of what happened in Nanjing. But I gleaned its seriousness at a young age through her unwillingness to set foot in a Japanese car or the way she would suck her teeth in frustrated response to Japanese electronics.

Unspent fury expelled itself in small bursts of con-
sumer protest. Po knew how to speak Japanese, but
never once did I hear it for myself.

I was twenty-two when I first sat down to learn
why, taking out a stack of books on the Second Sino-
Japanese War from the British Library. What they
contained made my hands tremble and my stomach
turn. I read them in the Social Sciences Reading
Room, taking a quiet desk near the back windows so
that when grief came I might feel some small sense of
privacy. The weight of it surprised me; the way words
about a massacre my grandmother's people endured
could fill me with rage and then a choking sadness.

There were grainy, faded pictures that showed the
women—those who hadn't made it out in time—
splayed open not just at their legs but at their guts,
babes in arms sliced the same. Bodies propped head-
less in the moments after their beheadings. Men half
buried in the ground to be mauled alive by dogs.
The photographs showed shoulders slumped over
bayoneted bodies, civilians raped and discarded for
sport. As I read the words Po could never articulate, I
scarcely touched the pages for fear of them.

But I kept note of two instances when Po revealed
her memories of that time. In one, she was running
across a field on a dry afternoon. The hum of planes

approached, and everyone hastened for cover. Po wore her bright orange qipao, and, afraid of being seen, no one wanted her near them. But she darted for shelter with the others, her dress like a signal flare rushing across the ground. My mother, when I recalled this story many years later, would shrug and say, "That's just like Po, though. She did what she wanted."

Her other memory I can stand to recall only in glimpses. Po and two women—strangers—picked their way across a ruined house. There was a noise, confusion, and the arrival of Japanese soldiers. Po took shelter on one side of the house, tucking down low behind a stone wall, and she was lucky. But she lived always with the sound of the other women's endings, the noise of soldiers and bayonets moving on soft bodies.

I cannot know the truth of it. The smaller calculations of war were not in those books. Po's stories aren't in the military records or in the diaries of the lauded Westerners who saved so many civilians. They exist only in that single moment when she opened her mouth and drew out an atrocity.

How do you corroborate a memory?

I GATHERED MAPS, MARKING HIS MOVEMENT across the middle reaches of China. I measured distances in the space between my thumb and index finger. From Shulu Old Village to Beijing, to Baoding, and to Shijiazhuang. I traced the route southwest to Guiyang and then toward Sichuan. I searched for maps from the period, wanting to know the roads he traveled. His letter unfolded a geography I would never know, a land he'd carried with him.

Whampoa Military Academy, the Republic of China's army training school, had relocated twice, from Guangzhou under Sun Yat-sen to Nanjing under Chiang Kai-shek and onward to Chengdu once the war with Japan had begun. Its movements mirrored the Nationalist government's, crisscrossing the country as political winds shifted, marking out an inverted triangle on the map, stretched across a vast distance.

My grandfather's was a generation that would never know rest. Years passed, and war continued.

China, having previously had little semblance of an air force, was reliant in the war upon a group of U.S. pilots known as the American Volunteer Group, the Flying Tigers. Gong was trained to fly with them. Everything—planes, weapons, people—had been put toward military efforts. It was a lean period for students: they learned on the equipment that was available. Gong wrote of his training as if it had been devised to sharpen his acuity. These memories were clear.

Once, flying solo, he was approached by another plane shortly after takeoff. In flying, he wrote, "The rules are always to be aware of your surroundings and never too close to another aircraft," so each time the plane approached him he pulled away. But the plane kept coming toward him, so, perplexed, he stayed in place, in case there was another reason the pilot wanted to pull so close. It was the flight instructor who'd chased after my grandfather to tell him that his right wheel had broken during takeoff. Calmly, Gong recalled his lessons on descending in rough terrain and landed on the one good wheel, damaging only a propeller of the plane.

After that incident, the group instructors favored

him. He was a good student and a reliable pilot. Two weeks later, during evening roll call, the instructors announced that the Air Force Commission was to award him thirty silver dollars. In his old age, in the thick of memory, he wrote amusedly that "to this day, almost sixty years later, I have not received this money."

The Flying Tigers were a popular success, garnering press attention and generating an allure for the skill of the pilots both in China and abroad. But China needed to strengthen its own air force; Japan's was formidable. In October 1942, the trainees boarded a C-47 transport aircraft, beginning a journey that would take them around the world. They flew first over the Himalayas, landing in Calcutta. It was treacherous crossing over "The Hump" of the mountains, the beginning of a lengthy journey across the Indian subcontinent to reach the Atlantic. After Calcutta, they took a train to Bombay, where they boarded an American naval cruiser headed for New York, zigzagging across the ocean to avoid U-boats. Long days were spent studying English and playing cards and nights in total darkness on board. Despite being at sea, they were unable to light even a cigarette for fear of attack.

From New York, they took a train to Arizona,

where a series of airfields had been put to use training foreign pilots. Gong was sent to Williams Air Force Base, thirty miles southeast of Phoenix, where he underwent advanced flight training, working with interpreters and American instructors. From Williams, he went on to Colorado to train on the plane he would pilot for the entirety of the war: the B-25 bomber.

In May 1943, he graduated from training and was sent to Miami, where he boarded a military transport to Brazil and then flew onward to Karachi. The Malir Airfield was the final training stop for Chinese pilots, where they would complete formation and combat training. The Chinese-American Composite Wing was activated in October of 1943, and Gong returned to China.

I began to search for records and history books to find evidence of the missions he flew. I wrote letters to veterans' groups and archives. Specifics were a challenge, but occasional dates, photographs, or footnotes presented themselves. Air force buffs on the internet offered details on planes, bases, and flight formations. A picture took shape of the months he spent at Liangshan Air Base, colored in by his words, by the heartbreak and exhaustion that would permeate his memories a lifetime later.

I found an old book on the Republic of China

Air Force with a foldout illustration of the B-25. The plane had space for a pilot, a copilot, and a bombardier, with gunners in behind. Online, I watched clips of vintage planes and U.S. Air Force training lessons from the war, likely the very films Gong had watched himself. The illustrations and videos gave details, but much of it remained meaningless to me. Without understanding the aircraft, I realized, I could not understand Gong's letter: Planes were as important as the terrain over which he flew. The language of manifold pressure and slipstream was opaque, but I savored the view of the cockpit, dials and levers forming a well-labeled landscape he knew well. In reading his words, I came to know the inner life of that confined space, when air was thin and even a minor mistake could have fatal results.

Liangshan Air Base was perpetually busy. Located in Sichuan, it was strategically vital, near to the edge of Japanese-controlled territory and roughly in the middle of China. From that central point, the air force flew missions to the eastern coast, to the north, and, on occasion, over Taiwan. Did Gong ever fly over the island that would become his home? It was his flights from Liangshan that he remembered most.

Having been solitary for so long, without family, the base brought him closer to others. He shared a dormitory with four other pilots in such proximity and constant pressure that, as he put it, "There was no time wasted in strife with one another." The realities of war dominated their lives.

In March 1945, the orders for what was viewed as a lengthy and dangerous mission came through. They were to target the railway running north to south from Beijing, picking away at its bridges and lines to disrupt transport routes. Escorted by fighter jets, bombers flew east to target the steel railway bridge stretching over the silt-filled Yellow River. The bridge was lined with antiaircraft guns; as Gong and his fellow soldiers flew out in formation, a third of their aircraft were shot down. Many died over the Yellow River: out of his five-man dorm, only two survived.

Days blurred in the close confines at Liangshan; nearing the end of the war, the bombers were kept busy, on long-stalled and often fatal missions, flying low through cloud and smoke to drop their payloads. The pain of it Gong remembered most: those who survived couldn't tell themselves apart from those who'd been lost to gunfire. Through misery and grief, the losses left the living, too, in a realm of the dead.

Death came close. Flying in diamond formation to bomb Japanese tanks, Gong piloted his B-25 over the searing plains of Henan. Hot air flows were common in the afternoons, and he needed to focus to tackle the thermal turbulence that resulted. The plane jolted in the air, and the bombardier became airsick, vomiting violently. The gunner in the upper turret rushed down to find out what was happening, and, furious at the commotion, Gong ordered him back to his position. At the very same moment, a metal clang sounded from the plane's walls.

They managed a landing, but after checks and re-hashing the flight with mechanics and intelligence officers, they discovered that the plane had been shot through by a Japanese antiaircraft bullet. The hole passed directly through the gunner's upper turret and out the other side, precisely where the man would have been seated had it not been for the commotion.

During the same months, flying out over Zhengzhou, Gong's plane battery died. The electronic indicators, meters, and controls failed. "All I could do," Gong wrote, "was rely on the P-51 fighter protecting me and land at the next airfield, at Xian, while my team flew on." It wasn't long before he received word that their team leader hadn't made it back to Liangshan, having crashed in the mountains. Heavy rain set in, so Gong and his crew waited, unable to fly back until a mechanic could be sent.

While Gong waited, the remaining five B-25s flew

on to Chongqing, where they refueled and loaded their bombs. All were lost over Sichuan on their return. Had it not been for Gong's malfunctioning battery, death might have come to him, too.

The war was closing, but the most brutal bombs were yet to come. By then, Gong would have traveled west once more.

His orders came first from Karachi: they were in need of a B-25 instructor. There, having escaped the fate of most of his fellows, having survived the war, Gong was offered a new position as a C-47 pilot for the air transport team, flying the leaders of Nationalist (Kuomintang) China from the air base in Shanghai.

Within the coming years of the civil war, Nationalist territory would be reduced. They would hold little more than an island off China's southeastern shore.

SHUI

n. WATER; RIVER

The Taiwan Strait is a turbulent border; but in migration, it is a corridor.

8

THE RIVERS SPREAD OUT TOWARD THE SEA, blue veins beneath digital skin. The map shows the crumple of mountains, then smooth plains, threaded through with water. I press my finger to each one, counting what I can. Too many, of course: 129, some too small to show at my distant resolution. I trace my nail over the ones I know, marking the drop to sea.

In the seventeenth century, that so many rivers could exist on such a small island elicited surprise from the newly arrived. The Qing official Yu Yonghe remarked that there were more creeks and gullies than he could possibly count, and that the journey from Tainan to the northern sulfur hills, past present-day Taipei, crossed some ninety-six rivers, many of which flowed fast and treacherous. By the nineteenth century, river travel had grown only marginally more placid: in 1864, the British biologist Robert Swinhoe reported to the Royal Geographical Society on an excursion along the Tamsui River in a flat-bottomed, shallow boat, occasionally tugged along on foot when the beds ran dry. But "after excessive rains and the melting of the snow on the mountains," he wrote, "the freshets convert the entire river into a large rapid, which drives everything before it."

I've traced river sources in a few places: on Hengchun, the southern peninsula; in the north at Huiyao, feeding the Keelung River; and in the high mountains at Nenggao. Now so many of the rivers stray from their courses, plugged and pooled in reservoirs or dried to dank beds awaiting the monsoon. Their innocent clarity grows turbid downstream, rivers thick with effluent, solvents, and waste flowing gape-mouthed to the sea. Water contamination remains high in the consciousness of Taiwanese environmentalists: though improved in recent decades, the state of the rivers deteriorated dramatically during the country's industrial-growth boom. In 1990, *The New York Times* reported that some rivers were so toxic as to be "pronounced dead." The rivers bore the weight of economic success. The majority of them are less than sixty miles long; pollution truncates their lives all the more.

From the peaks, though, they flow sweetly. The day we hiked toward Qilai on the Nenggao Trail, the sun had hung wanly amid the cloud. There remained a trace of warmth, so a group of us had stopped at a three-tiered cascade of white water, where a pool glinted at the base. We'd reached it by clambering down a small mound of rocks into a sheltered crevice of the mountain, which swallowed us with the sound of the Nenggao Waterfall. The tumble barely pattered the edge of the ice-green pool, and, elated at the thought of cold on my limbs after carrying my heavy pack up the mountain, I stripped down to my underwear and slipped in, shuffling my way across the rocky floor. It was deep, and I swam freely in the clean cold of it, some three thousand meters above sea level.

That water made its way to the basins below, forming a creek that fed the Wushe River, the Wanda Reservoir, and onward to the Choshui, Taiwan's longest river. The dividing line between south and north, the river traces a course westward, feeding the hydroelectric dam at Sun Moon Lake and irrigating the farm-rich flatlands toward the Taiwan Strait for rice, sugarcane, and watermelons. Nicknamed Muddy River, the Choshui carries so much sand that it regularly dries out, and dust storms have become a problem. It is badly impacted by the concrete industry and damming along its banks. But the water at its source is glass-clear.

In one legend, it is said that the river was once called Qingshui ("Clear Water") back when clouded leopards still stalked these mountains. A hill farmer had rescued a rabbit from the leopard's grip, and in return, the rabbit granted the farmer the gift of a wife. When this wife was attacked by a group of bandits, the farmer battled them over the cliffside and into the river to their deaths. With the blood of the bandits polluting its flows, the Qingshui became muddy. In another tale still fresh in the minds of locals, the muddy river would run clear at times of great social upheaval or disasters like quakes. It ran clear, the legend says, when Dutch colonists were defeated in the seventeenth century, and once more when the island emerged from Japanese rule in 1945. The natural world was a mirror to the islanders' fortunes.

On the Hengchun Peninsula far south, at Qikong Waterfall—Seven Holes—a flow descends a small, jungle-covered peak at the beginning of a mountainous break between the peninsula and the Central Mountain Range. The first pools in its lower reaches drain into a small creek and then into channels tunneling underground, rocky and unremarkable to look at, until flowing out to sea. The fourth "hole" of Qikong sits at a rocky ledge that drops sheerly to the pools below.

I remember swimming in that upper pool once on a visit with my mother and sister as rain fell onto the canopy trees. We settled by a milky blue-green pool, where an airy stream of water spilled from a ledge far above and spun down to the pool below. We plunged in together, a family bobbing in the barrel-shaped depths, the pool no wider than eight feet in diameter. The rock had been smoothed by an eternity of falling water, and a placid swimmer could rest on the polished stone and look out over the green valley below. Its wide and open sky was framed by hills, and the occasional bird caught wing in the white cloud. The autumn migration was near its close; we'd ventured south late in the season.

Swimming there, I saw joy on my mother's face: how much she must have missed in the years after she and my father divorced and my sister and I grew up, in the careful life she lived alone in Canada, going to work, running in the park, cooking simple meals for herself. I'd spent recent years collecting and examining old photographs of her, wondering if perhaps I could pinpoint our resemblance. As a small child, it had been there: my eyes were darker, my hair straight and long and black, my arms skinny like hers. I looked Chinese. In time, though, my shoulders grew broad, my cheeks red, my eyes light. I took the height of my Welsh relatives and now stand many inches taller than my mother. But beaming in that mountain pool, I shared her happiness, and I saw in her face something of my own.

•

FOR MANY PLACES, THE END OF THE SECOND World War meant rebuilding. In China it also marked a return to civil war, a return to the tensions that had raged since the end of the Qing dynasty and the May Fourth Movement. The Nationalists and Communists, who had united to fight the Japanese, resumed their positions as opponents.

Taiwan came once more under China's authority after five decades of rule by the Japanese. Inflation had plagued China since the 1930s and swelled rapidly after 1945, so supplies and goods from Taiwan were stockpiled and sent to the mainland. Bundles of yuan notes withered in value as soon as they were issued; money was better converted to commodities with a more stable value, like salt.

In some ways, in some places in China, a small

semblance of a previous life began to return. My grandmother started university in Nanjing in 1946, when Ginling Women's College resumed classes. She studied accounting, living for a brief period in her family home, the walls of which had survived the war, though the interior had been stripped bare, riddled with bullets, and damaged by smoke in the family's years away.

She then became a secretary at the air force headquarters and began dating a colleague who had relatives in Hong Kong. The Communists were winning the civil war, but Po's family was slow to realize their precarious position as wealthy landowners in a changing nation. In January 1949, though, like many government workers, Po arranged to leave Nanjing. A few days before her twenty-fifth birthday, she was to travel to Taipei to take up work at the air force base there in hopes of finding some refuge from the war.

She asked her parents to join her, but they were unwilling to go.

"Leave?" her mother cried. "We'll starve to death if we leave. We'll have nothing." Her parents did not believe what was, by then, evident to many. Thousands prepared to go, fearing the worst. Po's boyfriend fled to his family in Hong Kong.

With the privilege of hindsight, I wonder how a

family of merchants and landlords did not see what was coming. They had more resources than many. But Po prepared to depart alone, wearing a clutch of gold bars her mother had sewn into a belt for her. Arms in the air, my grandmother twirled as her mother wrapped the fortune doubly around her waist, securing it with a tidy pin, and then Po boarded a boat on the Yangtze River.

My mother told me the only story she had ever heard from her mother about that time.

The docks had been busy, so Po had arrived early, loading her luggage on the boat and finding her place amid the crowds on deck, ready for the journey. She didn't want to go, but having spent her days in government and military offices, relaying the messages of war, she understood why she had to. She waited, watching the people back on dry land, as other passengers boarded. She took a small comfort in company; a friend traveled with her, also bound for Taipei and the hope of security in Taiwan.

The throng of passengers and families parting—for a lifetime, though they did not yet know it—created such a noise that Po had to shout in conversation with her friend. They could hardly find space to stand. It is a wonder that Po saw the figure moving through the crowd, hobbling on bound and warped feet, clutching a tin of Danish butter cookies under one arm; the cookies were Po's favorite. It was, perhaps, an excuse to say goodbye again, to see her daughter once more. At the sight of her mother limping toward the river, Po panicked.

"I want to get off," she declared. "I want to stay."

Her bags were buried beneath the luggage of other passengers, and there was no chance of finding them. She darted to the boat's rail, desperate to make her way back to the dock, shouting to delay the departure.

"You'll never find your things," her friend told her. "Sail on. You can come back soon."

Her mother stood huddled on the dock, clutching the gleaming biscuit tin, watching while the boat prepared to depart. Futilely calling out to her mother amid the noise of the crowd, my grandmother watched the shoreline slip away. It was the last time she saw her mother and the last time she ever saw China.

HIS RECOLLECTIONS AFTER 1945 WERE NEBU-
lous. Paragraphs in Gong's letter seemed to reach
toward memories, only to find them incomplete,
without root. Sentences cut short, cycling between
glimpses of his time in the Civil Air Transport's
(CAT) VIP transport team—flying Nationalist officials between cities on the mainland—and moments
back in Karachi, training pilots on fighter jets in the
final months of the war with Japan. All this was scattered with references to earlier pages, passages, and
proverbs. He had been ill. In some sections, he was
in the burning haze of fever, believing he would die
from malaria, and in others he was lucid, morally
stoic. It was only with my mother's annotations that I
could assemble the story.

There were hints that things had soured within
the Nationalist government, that corruption was rife.

A friend suggested Gong write a contemporary take on *Officialdom Unmasked*, an inflammatory late-Qing novel about bureaucrats in the last days of the empire. But he wished solely to focus on the task of flying. He hoped to differentiate himself from his peers, not wishing to be tempted by the thrall of corruption, power, or money. "During those years," he wrote, "I came to know something about the personal lives of those I flew, but I did not wish to use bribery or succumb to greed, in damage to my conscience."

There was a saying in the CAT: "When the motor starts, gold bars abound." Flying black-market goods for profit was a lure to many.

"Why don't you do business, Tsao? Everyone else is," a pilot asked my grandfather.

"Nothing might come of other people's business, but if I do it, I may be locked up."

And later:

"Why don't you do business, Tsao?"

"I am afraid that greed would blind my conscience."

Near the end of this letter, Gong asked a question. "Was this period of my life like the proverb 'Life and death are a matter of fate. But riches and honors are determined by heaven'?" In 1947, he was transferred to a new air force post in Taiwan.

9

IN TAIPEI, OVER A DINNER OF FRIED NOODLES and braised cabbage, a friend of a friend introduces me to Charlene, a Taiwanese American cinematographer born not far from where my mother grew up. She has a wry sense of humor and the kind of detached attitude I often take for confidence. I learn that Charlene was raised in Taipei in the 1980s, in the decades after my family left. I feel drawn to her as if she holds some knowledge my family lacks. A part of me, too, envies Charlene those years here. I recognize in her the transience that has marked so much of my own life, navigating between worlds, in her case between LA and Taipei. Like me, she carries the traces of body and language that come from a life overseas, the markers of movement: in posture, in small gestures, in the volume of our voices. We who make our homes elsewhere give ourselves away in the little things we can't quite control.

Charlene tells me that though she often spends time hiking in California, she rarely ventures out in Taiwan. Some days later, on a dry morning, we meet for a journey east. We are intent on visiting Keelung Mountain, a grass-covered peak overlooking the northeastern coast, but by the time we dismount the coach at Jioufen, the sky is a heavy slate and fat drops of rain begin to fall. Tourists unfurl their umbrellas, winding their way through the awnings and up the narrow staircases of the village toward the food stalls, brightly lit in their rain ponchos. We stride onward, past the lanes, tying our hoods around our faces, our skin softening with the wash of water. At the base of the mountain, we check our laces and begin our route up the irregular stone steps, watching the rain pour down the hillside toward the harbor and the sea.

From the midpoint of the mountain, I can just about see Jioufen, the village on the hills, and Keelung's curving coastline, distant in a veil of rain. Pale lights twinkle in the gray, and fog blots out the borderland of the shore.

Between her curses about the incline of the steps, Charlene begins to distract me with tales of the food we can eat after our hike: feather-light taro balls and hot ginger soup, ice cream wrapped with peanut and coriander. Jioufen has become popular with tourists because of its lantern-lined alleyways, said to have inspired the Hayao Miyazaki film *Spirited Away*. In that story, when a girl loses her family she becomes a ghost herself.

The final flight of steps takes us through a mist so thick we cannot see each other. We walk directly into the rain cloud and emerge to white fog on the peak. Below us, a bed of clouds blocks the view of the sea below. The northeast is the monsoon corridor; the winter storm makes its way across the island from the East China Sea. Cold to the bone, we stand for a while, unseeing, cradled by cloud.

•

IT WAS AT KEELUNG'S PORT, WEST OF THIS HILL, that my grandmother arrived by boat in 1949, along with thousands of other mainlanders. In 1945, after the end of the Sino-Japanese War, Taiwan was returned to Chinese hands. It was at Keelung that Chen Yi, the Nationalist-appointed chief executive of Taiwan, arrived to govern the island. New arrivals like my grandmother would come to dominate the social and cultural life of Taiwan. Keelung thus ushered in the nation's changing fortunes, bringing ruin to some and prosperity to others. But after decades of Japanese rule—and after a war in which many Taiwanese were conscripted into the Japanese military—it would not be sufficient to claim that the island had simply been "liberated" from Japanese occupation, as some would say.

In those in-between years after 1945 and before the end of the civil war, tensions between mainland Chinese and the native Taiwanese grew strained. On February 28, 1947, government security fired shots into a crowd of protesters who were demonstrating against the violent encroachments of Nationalist rulers into daily life. The night before, a Taiwanese woman selling contraband cigarettes had been violently assaulted by state tobacco regulators. The incident—now known as the 228 Incident—spurred far-reaching violence. The tensions of the mainland civil war spilled over into Taiwan. As extra military forces were sent from the mainland, thousands of Taiwanese and newly arrived mainlanders labeled as Communists were executed or imprisoned by the Nationalist government, without trial and without warning. Political dissidents, intellectuals, and those accused of being Communist spies disappeared; Keelung Harbor and the rivers in Taipei flowed thick with bodies.

Taiwan's period of martial law under the Nationalists—spanning thirty-eight years—was the longest in human history. For many decades and throughout the time my grandparents lived and worked in the government and military, the freedom even to discuss what had taken place remained constrained. It did not change until the 1990s.

Yet soon after her arrival, my grandmother's life in Taipei took on some semblance of routine. She worked as a teleprinter operator for the air force, inputting and pulling communications from the telex, decoding their messages. She lived in a dormitory in Daan with other women from work and spent her free time at the popular air force bar, drinking whiskey to the tune of the American records so adored by the pilots, most of whom had trained abroad. She preferred Shanghai pop music and love ballads but was pleased, at least, to find some enjoyment during her rare evenings off.

But on the night of April 22, 1949, circumstances on the mainland changed dramatically as the Nationalist defenses of the Yangtze River near Nanjing fell. The government abandoned the city and fled the approaching Communist People's Liberation Army, which casually entered the city gate the next morning, declaring their takeover of China's capital at the time. Some reports say that the Communists had such an easy time taking the city, they needed to fabricate a grand entry for photographs a few days later.

The message arrived in Taipei on the telex lines, Nanjing's defeat simply typed in characters, printed on tape from an electronic reel. Po held the words in her hands, breathless, thinking of her mother hobbling to the docks just four months before. The office was in disarray as workers panicked; Po waited, desperate for news from her family, unsure of what to do.

The message finally arrived. Her mother wanted her daughter safe, so she suggested Po travel to Hong Kong, where her aunt and uncle lived. Obedient for once, Po booked her ticket, traveling the same week.

At this point in my grandmother's story, her memory grew vague. It is not a surprise; the turmoil of war was a source of great confusion in itself. She'd told me about her journey to Hong Kong six decades later, at a time when she was frequently undone by illness. Her eyes had misted with cataracts, her mouth had emptied of her yellowed teeth. How much could she remember of a life lived so long ago? How much would she truly want to share?

She told me she traveled to Hong Kong without notifying the air force, only to find that her aunt had moved to Shanghai. It was a baffling choice, as

Shanghai became embroiled in battle a month later and was ceded to Communist forces after a brutal defeat in June. Truly alone now, my grandmother traveled back to Taipei in September, later taking up a job as a secretary for the Nationalist leader, Chiang Kai-shek, at the Presidential Palace. And she was about to meet my grandfather.

•

CHARLENE AND I TAKE THE SMALL LOCAL train toward Wanggu, a single platform beside the broad path of the Keelung River. In recent days, the rain has lightened, but still mist patterns the north. Clad in our rain gear, we feel invincible. Sky lanterns from nearby Shifen—scrawled with the hopes and wishes of their senders—trace a slow fall toward the forest and are extinguished by the wind. We watch them from the bridge over the river as we walk the lanes south. The grace of their flight is abruptly broken by black smoke and their descent into the scenery: the hills are blanketed by the flaccid, chemically coated paper of these modern lanterns. The remains of wishes are strewn about, their paper and wiring in branches like garish birds' nests.

We follow the sound of water—rushing through

the patchwork rock, past the taro and rhododendron understory, through the damp of the northeast forest—to divine the locations of waterfalls. After a few miles up the curved, narrow road, we find a staircase, a clunky thing thick with algae, and lower ourselves down it. The rain has stopped, but the cascade makes a radio-static roar and sends more mist into the already damp world. Water flows over the base of the steps, which descend directly into the stream. Huiyao Waterfall erupts from the cliff above to land in a broad, roiling pool of turquoise. We find a flat rock on which to rest, and from here I undress to dip into the relative warmth of the stream.

We sit by the steps afterward, finding a silence in the movement of the water. The steadiness of the scene is broken only by the flight of a kingfisher, orange and teal against the white-hazed light.

During my doctorate, I carried out fieldwork at Hampstead Heath Ladies' Pond in London, and I interviewed the swimmers. So often, unbidden, they told me of their first kingfisher sightings. Many times, the kingfisher was the bird that had hooked them, taught them to love the pond. Though I swam there for years, I never saw one.

I watch as it hovers, electric, by the opposite bank of the creek. Charlene looks out toward the bird, but it flies off in a flicker of neon light. At this far end of my world, where the hills are so often washed to white, I laugh as I witness the kingfisher's flight at last.

•

IT WAS DURING THE RECORDINGS I MADE WITH Po that I learned, in her voice alone, of my grandparents' early years.

It was late 1949, shortly before the end of the civil war. It was a Saturday, the night when all the girls in the office went dancing. Po had plans to visit her friends, but the group of colleagues begged her to join them at the bar. She relented.

The girls flooded the dance floor, throwing themselves into the music, and my grandmother felt embarrassed. She settled alone into a seat at one end of the dance floor, watching them. Across the room, also alone, was Gong. With a boldness I struggle to reconcile with his shy character, he wandered over and asked her to dance.

"He wasn't a very good dancer," Po confessed. "But he was very funny."

My grandfather didn't talk much. He listened as Po told him all about herself. "I like to eat chocolate so much," she said, before sitting down to tell him about her work, her family, and all the things she liked to do. Then, without explanation, he got up and left.

Po's friends rushed over to ask what had happened. They all knew who he was: a team leader among the pilots.

"I don't know," Po began, unsure of where she had gone wrong. She returned to sipping her drink, watching her friends dance.

Half an hour later, Gong returned with an enormous bag of chocolates in all different shapes, some with nougat, some with caramel. He'd traveled to Hainan for work the day before, he explained, and brought them back with him.

He inquired if there was anything else she might want. He was going back on duty overseas in a few days and would happily buy what he could. But Po wanted nothing and was skeptical of his offer. The recent months sat bitter in her memory. Her friends enthusiastically placed their orders: wool fabric for dressmaking, sewing materials, and sweets.

A few days later, Gong returned, carrying a packet with several small lengths of fabric, a few for Po's friends and two that he'd chosen for her. Flustered, she told him that she couldn't pay for the fabric, as she didn't have much money. Some weeks before, having heard that her family back home was struggling to find enough food, she'd boxed up the gold bars her mother had sent with her and returned them by post to Nanjing. Gong's generosity seemed, to her, like stupidity.

"And I don't like air force pilots," she blurted out. "They're uneducated, and I don't want to worry about stupid men. I like bankers," she added conclusively.

Gong shook his head, explaining that he didn't want any money. In the weeks that followed, he called when he was in town, and they met for dinner. Eight months later, in 1950, in a quiet ceremony, they were married.

Their marriage brought them years together and years apart as military careers so often dictate. In the early days, before my mother was born, they lived in Gangshan, a district outside Kaohsiung, near the Air Force Academy, where Gong became an instructor. They lived in a two-story concrete building that had once served as Japanese military accommodations, with other flight instructors' families overhearing everything, living their lives in the public intimacy of the military village. The closeness must have been familiar to Gong. He painted the floors burgundy to brighten up the place and planted bananas in the garden. But in the newness of poverty, Po's resentment grew. They subsisted on a diet of rice and bean sprouts, only rarely affording a bit of tofu, meat, or eggs. "That is why," my mother once said, "as early as I can remember, Po never ate bean sprouts." I had laughed, recalling the steamer trays of shopping-mall food courts, the dank fried rice and soggy stir fries of suburbia. My entire childhood, I had believed that Chinese people didn't eat bean sprouts, that they were a filler added by chefs catering to North American tastes, when in fact, simply owing to Po's bitterness, they had been banished from our tables.

10

THE OLD SOUTHERN CITY OF TAINAN SITS
along a wide coastal plain. Once Taiwan's capital,
its streets are lined with historic temples, its shoreline with the remnants of fisheries. I've grown accustomed to thinking of the sea and sky as opposite
things, cut through by a border. But the western flatlands blur these boundaries. Where water breathes in
waves upon the shore, birds descend and speckle the
shallows.

Taiwan's biodiversity in plants and insects is mirrored by its birdlife. In the protected zone of Taijiang
National Park, on Tainan's western edge, white ibises,
Caspian terns, and whimbrels are commonly found
on the shoreline, a mid-migratory resting place at sea.
Less often, the dusty brown of the endangered spotted
greenshanks. And in autumn and winter, endangered

black-faced spoonbills gather in great flocks in the shallows.

Heat radiates from the road. It seems to catch the light, and the asphalt sags under the force of the sun. The air fizzles with the scents of sand, salt, and turbid water from the brackish shore. Exhaust fumes catch in the wind, a chemical note to a flatland perfume.

Mangrove forests line the inland waterways. The brittle seam between the mussel-shelled shore and the sea is elusive. Briny, interstitial things, on Taiwan's western coast mangroves are the last green thing before the strait sweeps out toward China. They are at the border of land and sea.

I feel the tidal pull of that in-between place.

Dense forest is absent in this part of the plains, hacked back and pushed inland centuries earlier. How different this place must have looked then. The jungle once grew thick to the shore, the mangrove belts clustered toward the acacia forests. Soapberries and fanflowers marked the coast, each band of forest a buffer between the sea and the mountains. By the time Robert Swinhoe traveled Taiwan in the 1850s, the territory was, he wrote, "almost entirely denuded of trees," with the cultivated plains vastly differing from the "primitive forests" in the mountains. Rough grasses had come in to cover the bare foothills, and instead of the deer and birdlife that graced the mountains, the plains boasted pigs and hares. The flat, well-watered lowlands were an agricultural Eden. Now the coastal forest is largely gone; the flatlands are mostly farms and fisheries.

But humans long for green, so the trees make their way back to the cities in ceramic pots and roadside verges, climbing the trellises of every back alley unabated. A few large banyans stand in the parks, offering meager shade. The blossoms grown in containers are abundant: bougainvillea climbs over the corners of buildings. Frangipani trees boxed into concrete cubes stretch out from the walls, their glass-green leaves a contrast to the road's dappled grays. Stray cats stalk around every corner, seeking the scraps of restaurants or the unseen bandicoot rats, which were brought here centuries ago by Dutch settlers.

•

I LACK THE PATIENCE NEEDED FOR BIRD-watching, but the evidence of birds can be seen everywhere: in fleeting song and fallen feather. In the cities, green patches are picked clean by the Taiwan magpie—the "long-tailed mountain daughter" in Chinese—elegant, blue-suited and black-capped, with a flame-red beak. Malaysian night herons stalk the parks at dusk, and songbirds in cages carry tunes into the alleys. With some luck, on the coast I hope to catch sight of the spoonbills. The city birds have made me optimistic.

It is December. Two months alone in Taiwan have given me some confidence. I decide to take a bike and wind my way through Tainan's sun-scalded lanes, past hawkers toasting egg waffles and spooning tapioca into tea. I pedal, lumbering amid the traffic. The bicycle is enormous, single-geared, and too heavy to maneuver. It takes me some time to find my rhythm, but eventually I settle, riding smoothly, my breath heavy. Wind has moved into the lowlands overnight, and even before waking I could hear the windows rattling in their frames. Out on the road, it is no better. Dust flies as much from the surrounding masses of scooters as from the gusts, so I put on sunglasses to shield my eyes and hope that the wind will abate.

Six miles on, at the edge of Tainan, the buildings peter out. The city hunches down near the water, becomes a half-choked pattern of reservoirs, lagoons, and canals, unfolding toward the sea. The ground is cut through with lanes, mudflats, and the small tracks left by skittering crabs. At Taijiang National Park, the spoonbills follow the tide. I checked the forecast before leaving, and high tide will arrive at noon.

I reach the shore, where the shallows are lined with bamboo rafts for harvesting oysters. I pause where the waves pummel the gray, and a pair of fighter jets rip overhead. Their tinned sound announces their arrival a second out of step, and the noise draws my gaze skyward. Their paired flight will repeat intermittently throughout the day, their drone a call to remembrance. My grandfather flew here through the 1950s and '60s. This coastline, facing out toward the continent, still has daily patrols.

Just as quickly, the sound of the jets is swallowed by the sounds of cicadas and the wind. I've begun to sink into the damp sand, so shake my feet free and shove the bicycle off the tiny strip of beach, back onto the asphalt. An enormous bridge spans the broad mouth of the Sicao wetlands where they meet the sea, and weekday fishermen gather to chew betel and tend their lines, which are dropped steeply over the edge. Chasing the tide, I cross over, reaching the invisible border between the city and the waterland that lies ahead.

•

TAIJIANG NATIONAL PARK IS AN ODDITY BY ANY measure: a collection of aquaculture reservoirs, salt pans, estuaries, and the Cigu Lagoon—an inland sea that once made the area ideal for anchoring ships and establishing fisheries, but which, like many of Taiwan's wetland ecosystems, has diminished drastically over time. I repeatedly scrolled across the blue of the map in the weeks before visiting, wondering what a landscape made of water and stitched with such fine seams of green might be like, the satellite view giving me little more than a tourmaline swirl. But cycling in, I find there is little fanfare on arriving at the national park, little to make it known that the park exists at all.

I follow the coastline on a marked bicycle track running between the checkerboard of fish reservoirs and the sea. Decaying buildings dot the grid. Empty blue plastic drums lie overturned, and the remnants of ropes and plastic ties litter the small tracts of land running between the reservoirs. These estuary lands have long been used for fisheries, and the park emerged not long ago as a way of securing the future of the coastland in the face of industrial development. The Taijiang flats tell a story of fish, birds, plants, and people.

In the seventeenth century, foreign powers began to scramble for a foothold on the island. Before Qing soldiers claimed the island, in 1624 the Dutch East

India Company settled at Anping, eventually naming it Fort Zeelandia, and used the west coast as both a defensive stronghold and trading point. During decades of violent attempts to subdue the local indigenous populations and to oust the Spanish, who held forts in the north, the Dutch introduced the long silver-green milkfish, following cultivation methods from Indonesia. The region became known for the delicacy, with locals developing a taste for the fish steamed, fried, or stirred into rice porridge. When the Ming loyalist Koxinga and his troops arrived almost forty years later and laid siege to the Dutch, legends say they were greeted with placatory gifts of milkfish. Milkfish cultivation was extended through a series of ponds, as well as inland salt pans.

In shaping the world, humans shape the futures of fellow species. More than half the global population of black-faced spoonbills now gather for winter at the Tsengwen Estuary at Taijiang because the birds have long taken to the spoils of the fisheries, with a taste for the small fry and shrimp dwelling in the muck of shallow milkfish ponds. However, decades of industrial encroachment—and the turning over of many ponds to deep-water species—spelled a threat to the spoonbills. In the early 1990s, the species was facing severe population decline, and with just three hundred of them left, they were listed as critically endangered.

Of the six spoonbill species in the world, the black-faced spoonbill is the only one facing such threat. They wade in landscapes to which humans cannot go: many of the birds find a home in the de facto nature reserve of the demilitarized zone of the Korean Peninsula, breeding in the summers in the coastal flats made habitable by a lack of human encroachment. From there they make their flight southward. They trace the coastlines of East Asia, wintering over in Taiwan and Hong Kong. Of the patchy and political contentions of human life, the birds take no notice. As the Taiwanese poet Liu Ka-shiang writes, they are "the North Forest / Roosting on southern seashores." Nature stitches a seam between our anthropogenic divides.

In 1994, the same year the spoonbill was listed as critically endangered, Tainan residents gathered to protest a proposed industrial park and plans to erect a naphtha plant, a steel mill, and a petrochemical factory.

After nearly two decades of campaigning, political wrangling, and public debate, Taijiang eventually became Taiwan's eighth national park, extending from as far north as the salt pans at Cigu to the southern wetlands at Sicao. With the birds' feeding ground in the muddy tidal flats of the estuary secured, their populations have rebounded dramatically. Some four thousand black-faced spoonbills were counted in the 2017 survey.

This western shoreline still faces drastic transformations. The Cigu Lagoon was once an inland sea large and deep enough for Dutch ships to anchor, but much of it became choked with mud during either torrential rains or an earthquake in the early nineteenth century. By the mid-nineteenth century, British geographers canvassing the terrain complained of the shallowness of Taiwan's ports, noting that boats were compelled to anchor some two miles offshore. Today the lagoon exists at the whims of the tide. The Tsengwen River runs down from the Alishan Mountains, tracing the journey to sea level from the middle heights of the island. But the outwash of sand is largely prevented by damming upstream. While sand would once flow out and form stretches of coast, the process of wetland creation has been stalled. Sea levels are rising, and the coastline, instead of growing with the sediment of a free-flowing river, is shrinking.

Wetlands like Sicao provide a crucial flood break, forming a barrier to storm surges. Mangrove forests and wetland plants serve also as carbon sinks, where carbon accumulates in the mud of tidal forests over thousands of years and is all too easily released when the forests are cleared. As with the spoonbills, the forests need space. Building near the shore prevents the mangroves' march inland. With too much coastal development, the forests wither; too great a rise in sea level, and the forests drown. The mangroves' existence is interstitial, edgy, and precarious.

Climate change compounds Taiwan's predicament with typhoon rains and winds, mudslides, floods, and quakes. Seaside temples and grave sites on the western coast have begun to overflow with seawater. More worryingly, much of the island's chemical industry sits on this vulnerable low-lying shore, and Taiwan's largest coal power plant, near Taichung, has long been the world's largest emitter of carbon dioxide. This small stretch of receding ground shelters a contiguous array of petrochemical industries, farms, cities, and birds such as the spoonbills. The mangroves cannot hold our inheritances at bay.

•

LIKE A DIVING BIRD I CARRY ON, SURFACING EV-ery so often from the focus of cycling to cast my gaze across pools and clusters of mangroves. The salt smell of the waves is pervasive. It deadens the sulfur stench of the mangroves, which spring up every so often in deep-green clusters. The hot air feels thick with the fine-milled scent of sand, cut through with whiffs of rotted fish and sea breeze. Past the green tunnel, the canals are lined with round leaves, and I wonder, if I could take to the water, what emerald shades might glint within them.

I take a turnoff that leads inland, buffered between reservoirs and the battered shelters that dot the park. Bollards have been erected along the water. From atop my bike, I can just see over them, out toward the strait, where white waves break limply over the shallows and sandbars once softened the force of the westward sea. It looks more tranquil than I expected—glittering gray and fish-scale silver—with the tide on its way out.

Darting between the ponds, I keep one eye trained to the periphery, watching. The lanes are narrow, but not unmanageably so, with just the occasional turn between the squares of swamp green. Above most of the ponds, gulls take lazy turns on the wind, catching currents like pilots, watching for the occasional fish to dart airborne from the depths of the reservoir murk. The fighter jets return every so often, too.

It is against a verdurous wall of shrubs that I see

them. I halt my bike suddenly but quietly, not wanting to make a sound. I have cued myself to spot white, the birds being identifiable by their white plumage and black, scoop-shaped bills. These birds, white-plumed and black-billed, are clustered in a sea break of trees. Not quite right. I pull out my phone and check the list of birds I saved the night before: black-headed ibises. They sit unperturbed atop a wind-sculpted casuarina, which droops comically under their weight. A few yards away, black-winged, red-legged stilts wade in the shallows. All are soon besieged by a mass of their fellows dancing gracefully along the water's margin. Like a parabola sketched into the sky, they rise and then descend in unison, a faint reflection looping in the glaucous pool beneath. I watch them awhile, snapping a useless photograph—their dance too swift for my amateur lens—and then cycle on, delighted at least to have seen life amid the concrete-dusted ponds and graying sea. But not yet spoonbills.

The canal running inland smells of salt, and along this stretch of concrete road I feel I am baking in the winter sun. On my map, there is no crossing for a few miles, so I push on, noting that I've been out for nearly three hours. The tide will turn soon. I count the streaks of color and light—egrets, cormorants, terns—and am relieved, halfway up the road, to come to a steel bridge, shining new, its road fresh with the dust of construction. I stop to decipher a sign and get as far as the date: the bridge opened just yesterday. The map on my phone shows my pulsing blue presence, but no bridge. Grinning, I cycle its unrecorded length, appearing to the satellites, I imagine, as if in flight, flitting across the surface of the water, across the gap between our simulated and material worlds.

The ponds and roads on the other side are sparser than I've seen so far, and I wonder momentarily if I am on the right track. I take a left turn where my map shows a skinny track of green but find a small wharf and a canal; there is no path to the next grid of ponds. I track back, passing the steel bridge once more until the next turnoff northward. Tsengwen is still a short distance away, and my mouth is drying with thirst.

I pause to sip from a carton of iced tea, now warm from the sun, and a mechanical rumble approaches from behind. A man on a scooter greets me with a red-toothed smile. His arms are thick and beaded with sweat, and a towel the same cobalt blue as his shirt covers his head. His waders are still wet with muck from the ponds. Alone, taken off guard, I hesitate. He speaks to me in Mandarin, chewing betel nut between phrases.

"Ni yao qu nali?"

I sigh in relief. These are words I understand. "Where are you going?" I begin to explain, in muddled phrases, that I am looking for spoonbills but stop halfway as I realize I don't know the word for them. Instead, I emphasize the word niao ("bird"), miming a broad bill. I flap my arms once or twice and then wait, half embarrassed, for his reply.

He laughs, then tells me to be careful. Up ahead— he points along the road—are dogs, gou, another known word. Putting his scooter in gear, he says that he'll ride next to me until we pass them. They are known to chase passersby, he says, but these wild dogs all know him. I feel puzzled by the situation— knowing that in any other place I'd be skeptical of such an offer—but nod my head in agreement. We begin to ride in parallel, him shouting questions over the clicking sound of the scooter, and I answer where I can, explaining away my poor Mandarin when I can't.

"How have you ended up here looking for birds?" he asks. With my limited ability, I explain that there aren't many of them left in the world. Meiyou duoshao. I emphasize each syllable. He points backward, toward an elaborate temple that he thinks I'd like better. The birds, he says, are hard to see.

We pass the dogs, who bark once or twice and trot

curiously to the edge of the road before turning back, indifferent, and then we come to the main road. A heavy concrete lorry races past, leaving me coughing in its sputtered wake. The man points out the direction of the temple once more, turns right, and then waves goodbye. Two more lorries rumble past, and I hesitate, a bit defeated, unsure I want to take this dusty, busy road. But I've cycled a long way and seen only a handful of the birds I hoped to see. I resolve to give it a go and find my place on the shoulder of the road. I pedal fast to keep pace with the traffic.

I spot the shape across two lanes of cars, a flicker of white amid the slate tinge of a shallow pond. I brake suddenly, sending a cloud of dust into the air behind me and wait for a lull in the traffic before darting across. There is a grassy ditch next to the reservoir where I leave my bike, and I make my way toward the water. Standing still, I watch the bird some forty yards away. It stoops its head low, digging in the mud, working its way across the shallows. It swerves from side to side, a bobbleheaded dance, and I am sure. Crooked black legs step awkwardly through the sand. It stands alone, not in the crowd I imagined, swaying and swiveling its bill in the ground, coming up momentarily, allowing me a glimpse of its entire face. A black bill with a rounded scoop at its base, the broad curve is unmistakable even at this distance. A black-faced spoonbill.

I watch, riveted, as unperturbed by the passing traffic as this lonely seabird seems to be. It works its way across a section of the pond, feeding thoroughly before tracking back, covering a distance no greater than nine meters. In the far corner of the pond, an egret watches, awaiting the moment to dip in and feed as well. The pond has been almost completely emptied, part of the agreement between the fishermen and conservationists hoping to create a better habitat for the spoonbills when the milkfish cultivation is ceased in winter.

I raise my lens and snap a photograph, frowning at the blurred spot of white that appears in the viewfinder. But I feel the glow of satisfaction as much as the exhaustion in my legs. The heavy rental bike rattles on its kickstand with every passing truck. But I fill myself with glimpses of the wader.

GONG'S LETTERS NEVER MENTIONED MY GRAND-
mother. It was a conspicuous absence, as if in its pages
he'd sought to blot out something that he had carried, unhappily, for many decades. They had never
been close; they rarely ate together and spent their
time in opposite corners of their small bungalow. Po
had taken the larger room, and Gong took the tiny
room in the back. When she spoke—in haranguing
bursts—he remained silent.

In the decades after my mother was born, she and
my grandmother moved to Taipei, where Po worked
as a government secretary, to the small apartment
in Daan District. But during the school holidays,
my mother would visit Gangshan Air Force Base to
stay with my grandfather. For a time, he was based
at Chiayi—where the mountains rise to a spine—and
then later, in the 1960s, at Hsinchu, on the northwest

coast. At Hsinchu, he absorbed himself in the daily needs of the pilots, counseling them and offering guidance. In this way, two decades passed. In his letter, he wrote almost nothing of this time, until the end.

I saw a photograph once, taken while he was stationed at Gangshan, training F-100 pilots. He stood in front of a fighter jet, clad in a flying suit and flight pack, helmet in one hand. His face appeared expressionless at first glance, but looking closer, I could see it. The tiny curl of a smile, the furrow in his brow. In flying, perhaps, he found something of comfort.

A few years back, I flew over China on a clear day during a flight to Taiwan. I awoke to bright sun on the copper-tinged slopes beneath, and I could see rivers trace their courses through the arid land. I tried to place Gong—a lifetime ago—in the air, flying a route he had known well. How strange it felt, to fly over this place to which our family had once belonged. I realized, then, the magnitude of that loss: for Gong to never set foot on such territory again.

But just once, before the end of the civil war, before he had left for Taiwan, my grandfather had seen his home from the air:

> When I was stationed in Shanghai with the CAT, every time I flew from

Shanghai to Beijing, or from Beijing to Shanghai again, I had an indescribably strange feeling. There was a point in flight when it would occur. I suspected for a long time that it was our old family homestead. Just once, when there were no passengers on board, I dove down to see if it truly was our old home, our old village.

I descended from eight thousand feet to three hundred, and it became clear that it was our home. Our house in the east, facing the west. A small temple in the south and the locust tree. Our field on the edge of the village. And to the northeast, our family graves, our ancestors, and our loving mother.

Mother's love was engraved on my heart. I have since felt dissatisfied with all others. It is as Yuan Zhen wrote:

曾經滄海難為水
除卻巫山不是雲

I am dissatisfied with all water, having seen the depth of the ocean, and with all clouds, having seen the clouds on Wushan.

I teared up thinking of mother's love—my first love—and my guilt at not being able to fulfill my duties to her. Unable to return, unable to care for our ancestors' tombs. I felt the torment of Confucius's phrase:

樹欲靜而風不止
子欲養而親不在

The forest wants to be still, but the wind will not relent. The child wants to care for its parents, but the parents are gone.

11

WHEN I WAS THIRTEEN, MY GRADE-EIGHT English class was assigned William Bell's *Forbidden City*, a young adult novel that follows a Canadian boy as he accompanies his cameraman father to document the demonstrations at Tiananmen Square. It was the first and only book we read in school that documented the culture from which my family came. I read it rapt, staying up late into the night turning the pages. I wondered if the other two Chinese students in my class felt the same, but they came to lessons with the same quiet, adolescent disinterest as usual.

It was not my family's story. I had never been to China, knew little of it, and knew that we were somehow different from the other students whose families had emigrated from the mainland. My family had left China and been unable to return.

A lifetime later, the letter and the phone bill were what remained. One number in Taiwan, one number in China.

My mother dialed the Chinese number repeatedly for months, getting no answer. Often, the call wouldn't connect, but still she called, just to see. After two months, the call went through and a woman named Dong-ping answered.

My mother had never heard of Dong-ping, but they began, haltingly, to learn of each other's lives, pulling the frayed threads of their shared history; Dong-ping was my mother's cousin, my grandmother's niece.

What my mother feared most was confirmed: coming from a wealthy family of landlords, Po's sister and her husband, both teachers, had been denounced as capitalists and counterrevolutionaries. They were sent to labor camps like so many who toiled and died under long sentences in remote parts of the country. Their properties had been confiscated, the businesses closed. I thought of the way my grandmother had listed them, counting them on her fingers, and wondered how much else she might have hesitated to say. In those years, Dong-ping lived with her grandparents—Po's parents—in Nanjing.

For four years after her daughter left Nanjing,

Po's mother hobbled to the end of the road, every day awaiting her return. Each afternoon, Po's father sat with a Danish butter cookie tin on his lap. Inside it was a stack of photographs: pictures of Po throughout her childhood. Of Po's three siblings, one was denounced; one committed suicide; and one, her younger brother, survived.

The mainlanders who fled could not return to the country they had known; for decades, travel between Taiwan and China was banned. Many took shelter in Taiwan in the belief that they might one day be restored to their homeland. It was a potent but brutal dream: the Nationalist state supplanted much of the complexity—linguistic, cultural, and intellectual—that had for so many centuries distinguished Taiwan from its neighbors. Any illusion of the possibility for self-determination or democracy for the island dissolved. Taiwanese and Japanese languages were forced out of daily use, and once more Taiwan faced a rewriting of history: its legacies now belonged to China, to a motherland across the strait to which no one could even go, but to which they were told they would be rightfully restored.

Political migrants. Exiles. Colonists. Diaspora. The past has many words for my grandparents' generation, all of them containing a grain of the truth.

In recent decades, anthropologists and sociologists have attempted to make sense of their dislocated identity. 籍貫 jiguan ("identity based on one's family's native province") remained a legal means of categorizing identity until 1992. But many descendants of mainlanders—in my mother's generation and thereafter—have increasingly identified as both Chinese and Taiwanese, or some as Taiwanese alone.

A reluctance to relinquish ties to past places and the reality of seven decades severed from the mainland complicates what ought to be simple: articulating who we are.

Our versions of the truth so often dwell in the language we choose, but the words we use have consequences: they signify allegiances, shared histories, harms, and losses. In my childhood I heard phrases like "Taiwan, the true China" or "Chinese, but from Taiwan," and rarely felt pressed to make sense of them. The task of naming so often exceeded me. Instead I felt a discomfort, like an amorphous thing. My complacency, I know now, was a privilege afforded by distance, by the ease of light skin and features that passed for whiteness. I do not know why we did not visit Taiwan during my childhood, and I never asked. Instead, I negotiated the world as a dual citizen of Britain and Canada, casting my life in those frames of reference. The question of whether to call myself Taiwanese or Chinese felt a complication too far. I often found myself with too many names, too many homes, and no fixed sense of which order to arrange them in. A use of just one was an erasure of another. For most of my life—until Gong's Alzheimer's, until his death—I gave it little thought.

In the 1980s, the travel ban between Taiwan and China was finally lifted. Still my grandparents did not go back; after the civil war, it seemed that the old country they had left, the homes to which they hoped to return, no longer existed. My grandmother never spoke of her wounds, but they were there, in raw words. My grandfather's family had scattered long before 1949, and no nationalism could have rectified that. The home to which he longed to return was the hearth where he cooked by his mother's side as a child. He had lost that long before.

Much of what I've learned of the past I gleaned from books, from novels and historical studies. Families remain silent so often, and often understandably. But in those few recordings of my grandmother, and in the erratic lines of my grandfather's letter, the past transmuted into something personal, painful. In Taiwan I seemed to carry their haunting inside, ready to inhabit the places I found.

•

AFTER SIGHTING THE SPOONBILL, I RETURN TO the courtyard house where I've taken a room for a few days. The house stands at the end of a quiet lane in Tainan's university district, three stories tall with a narrow staircase to the rooftop, where the streetlights shine at eye level. I sleep, the wind still rattling the window frames, and I dream of white-winged birds. They have turned, in the way that dream creatures often do, into other things: powdered wings of sugar, mounds of sweet cream. I am in the pink-walled bakery in Niagara Falls where my grandmother took me as a child. She stands admiring a doily-lined tray of cream-puff swans. Their hooked necks sit golden above their bodies—the birds static in a refrigerated landscape—perched on the golden ground of a bakery tray. She hands me one, smiling, and I wake.

The house is quiet. Five o'clock and the morning has barely spread its blue warmth through the sky. I reach for my camera, to study once more the smudge of white against the blue that I know to be a spoonbill. I zoom in until I can just see the dark curve of its bill. It traveled a thousand miles to overwinter in those muddy pools.

A gateway to the island, the Tainan area gazes

out over the strait, beneath the westernmost nose of the island, raised toward China. Political and military tensions now choke the strait, but nature alone once sufficed to make crossing the Black Ditch a risky endeavor. When ships first ventured to the coastal islands beyond China, sailing the strait could be treacherous. Fog would set in and swells would rise around ships.

I often think of the myth of the sea goddess Matsu. Her legends took many forms, shapeshifting like a turbulent sea. In one popular account, the young girl Lin Mo was born to a family of Fujianese fishermen. At the temple one day, she was given the gift of future sight by the goddess Kuan-yin. Lin Mo's powers grew, until she began to predict the tides and the storms that raged off her coastal island. One day while weaving, she saw a vision of her father and brother drowning amid a tempest. She fell into a trance that enabled her to reach and rescue them from the sea. But the girl's mother, seeing her asleep at her loom, shook her awake too soon. The father drowned.

In another tale, she waited on the shore in a red dress, drawing sailors back to safety like a beacon. In another, she drowned after swimming for days to find her missing father, and was celebrated by her village for her filial piety. In Yu Yonghe's version of the

Matsu legend, she would fly to the sea in her dreams like a bird, saving drowning sailors. It is said that in death she climbed the highest mountain, ascending to the heavens encircled by fog.

In every story, Matsu was a young woman who faced the waves. Matsu dwelt in a peripheral space, in the sea between, until she was swallowed into fog. A swimmer myself, I feel drawn to her.

Down a back alley in the town, in the early morning, I cross over a construction site, through a narrow lane, and find Matsu's temple, buttressed with steel girders, cast in shadow. The doorway is painted with fading murals, and darkness shrouds the sanctum. The shadows are broken only by a lit altar where Matsu sits, cast in gold and aglow. I stand in the temple studying Matsu's serious gaze, her broad cheekbones glittering gold, her image framed in light. A young-girl savior worshipped by rough-tongued sailors, Matsu is so venerated that Taiwan has nearly a thousand temples devoted to her.

The shining mudflats I saw at Taijiang reach out into the water, speckled with the migrant birds that seek these shores each winter. Do the seabirds fly above the strait as Matsu once did? I once saw a map of spoonbill migration corridors with cartoonish arrows lining the coasts of China, Japan, Korea, and Taiwan, over the East China Sea, toward the strait. Wading the salt flats, the records of their movements on land wash out with every turning tide. The birds' survival is predicated on migration by flight through these fraught places. For them, like Matsu, the dark waters of the Taiwan Strait are no barrier. They are a corridor, a passage between seasons, salt-soaked and sunlit.

•

ON A WHIM ONE AFTERNOON AT THE LIBRARY in Berlin, I'd called up a stack of Chinese and Taiwanese literature. I'd been curious, perhaps, because my grandfather's letter had been interspersed with quotations and imagery from texts he'd studied in his youth, the florid inflections of Chinese language that I would never learn in my perfunctory, childlike Mandarin. Names appeared every so often—Yuan Zhen, Shen Kuo—and the text was laced with untraceable proverbs. I was stunned by Gong's sponge-like ability to carry names and aphorisms, to reference long-dead painters and philosophers in everyday correspondence. Within the limits of our language barrier, I had never heard him speak in borrowed words. Our conversations were basic and domestic: the language of cooking and mealtimes, of grandparents offering affection. He had said only as much as was needed. I hadn't seen many books around him in his old age. But somehow those old phrases stayed with him as his mind corroded. I read the books greedily— their words a corrective—and began to plot out a list of texts in translation to work through.

There were those that dwelt in the world of nature, like *The Classic of Mountains and Seas*, which was written around the fourth century B.C.E., remained popular through two millennia, and has been read variously as mythology, cosmology, and fiction. Throughout the first millennium, it was viewed by many as a *descriptio mundi*, a valid geographical survey of the world: indeed, the *Classic*'s unknown author was in some sense a well-traveled naturalist or was at least advised by locals from all regions of China. It was in such texts that a notion of Chinese territory was explored, with regions both "within" and "beyond the seas," as Taiwan once was. The *Classic* was a trove of botanical and zoological knowledge, with species so strange as to be of myth or others documented in its pages and now extinct, unrecorded, or otherwise unknown to us in the present. It catalogued plants that could stop swelling, blossoms that could prevent you from going astray, some for virility, some for good hearing, and it laid out a topography of a land long in the past, with mountain ranges scattered with unknown fauna. Though a far cry from what we might call science today, the book gleamed with inklings of a scientific method in the making.

In *Brush Talks from Dream Brook*, sometimes translated as *Dream Pool Essays*, written by Shen Kuo in the Song dynasty around 1088, I found a miscellany of observations of the natural world: the movements of celestial bodies, river types, and the etymology of words used to describe them. Shen preceded modern geology with his studies of stones. He wrote of petrified plants and fossils, of magnetism and the poles, of the shadows of hawks and how they shift with the movement of the sun.

In one passage, he told the story of a cluster of mollusks brought up from the riverbed by a fisherman, layered like fish scales into a solid shape. The fisherman pried open the shells and found inside a pristine copy of the *Buddhist Diamond Sutra*, a book of spiritual discourses. The pages had survived the river in their calcified cage. I thought, reading this, that our fleeting human worlds are so easily swallowed up by nature, our fate fastened to its course. What we believe to be culture is only ever a fragment of natural world that we have sectioned off, enclosed, pearl-like, for posterity.

I turned then to the nativist literature of Taiwan, which first emerged in the 1920s, in response to Japanese rule, as a means for preserving links to the Chinese languages. I found in these modern works that to speak of Taiwanese literature is often to speak of the landscape: the island's literature, from both indigenous and Han Chinese perspectives, has long been preoccupied with the land, with the mountains and forests that form the backdrop for the cities below. The nativist movement subsided in the war years only to reemerge, shapeshifted in the 1970s, as a form of resistance to Chinese Nationalist rule. Alongside it was the Tangwai opposition movement, which sought political representation amid a system in which opposition parties to the Kuomintang were forbidden; it resulted in the creation of Taiwan's Democratic Progressive Party.

Literature has since become a means of asserting the island's distinct cultural identity, in direct contention with its difficult colonial past. Rejecting the notion of Taiwanese literature as mere "frontier" writing, authors in a new tradition pursued their autonomy as part of their writing. In efforts to de-sinicize the island's identity, the Japanese colonial period was a point from which to argue that the island's cultural heritage diverged from China's. Such literature would be marked by its engagement with political struggle, with democracy, and with nature.

•

ONE MORNING I FIND MYSELF AT THE NATIONAL Museum of Taiwan Literature, off a busy roundabout in central Tainan. I've come to see the permanent exhibition on the history of Taiwanese literature but instead see a large banner in the front hall, forest-hued, pointing to a darker, much smaller hall. It is a special exhibit on Taiwanese nature writing.

Inside is a plethora of work far from the nature-writing traditions I know, tracing a lineage to nature writing in the United States. There are echoes of Carson and Thoreau but few of British Romanticism. I find in Taiwanese nature writing rather realist worlds, with essays, poems, and stories tied inextricably to activism. The words I read are subtle but matter-of-fact, not elegiac, though they so often deal with loss. Emerging in 1981 with the writers Han Han and Ma Yigong's "We Have Only One Earth" (我們只有一個地球), the genre's early texts tackle the scale of environmental loss on the island. Drawing deeply on the natural sciences and written at a time when forestry had all but devastated Taiwan's hills, when cities were growing apace, the early works contain an energy quite unlike the sweetened prose I've grown used to in British nature writing.

It was protest and activism that enabled the protection of the wetlands, something that in my grandparents' time in Taiwan would have been impossible. In the period of martial law, from 1949 to 1987, the very act of bird-watching could have brought you trouble, the use of binoculars an accusation of espionage. But following the turn to democracy—which arose in parallel to protests for democratization elsewhere in South Korea and in China at Tiananmen— activism driven by local communities thrived. The end of martial law created an opening for a burgeoning environmental movement, particularly as economic development was increasingly shaping public planning across Taiwan. Conservation and bird-watching societies formed, and writing that tackled both nature and activism flourished.

After the museum, I read what I can track down, writing to translators of local authors, finding so little Taiwanese nature writing that has made the journey into English. I am wholly absorbed. The contemporary Puyuma indigenous author Badai tells stories of millet fields grown on ancestral lands sold to city strangers and of river floods and the trees farmers use to document the rising waters. I search for the poems of Liu Ka-shiang, one of Taiwan's leading contemporary nature writers, and the novels of the lepidopterist and literature professor Wu Ming-Yi. In their pages, the minutiae of the mountains dwell in words.

In his 1984 poem "Small Is Beautiful," Liu Ka-shiang traces the journey of the Dadu River upstream. There are sandpipers, snipes, and ducklings at the river's mouth, egrets and the crowding of factories and waste. His river carries ever backward, upward, past swallows and kingfishers, river birds darting through the leaves of the thickening woodland. The poem reaches the mountains—the water's source—and once more there are the river's sandpipers. Liu writes that grouped everywhere along its waters, they find their place together, "Using themselves as the center of their living territory, / Crying, guarding, / telling the world that the stream beneath the wide-leaved woods is their home."

I feel a flush of envy for the sandpipers. These birds that exist on the page—and indeed, the space between real and poetic birds is vast—call the length of the river home. Their territory is demarcated, and their river is the poem: they appear where the stanzas open to the sea, and once more at their source, near the poem's close. But I know too that these birds—common sandpipers and wood sandpipers and others, Liu does not say which he means—live beyond the page. Sandpipers work their way over nearly all our world, save the coldest and the driest places (they are found neither in Antarctica nor in deserts). Tied to water, sandpipers move with the tides.

Along the East Asian–Australasian Flyway, more than five hundred species migrate. The route spans the thousands of miles between the Arctic—from Alaska to Russia—and New Zealand, taking in the entirety of the East Asian shore. The birds that travel its currents find regularity in their seasonal movements, though their coastlines are changing, whether from wetland encroachment, climate change, or industrial development. As with the spoonbills, the fortunes of migrant birds are tied to ours: to our abilities to protect them, to our willingness to afford them space in our worlds, to offerings that were never ours to give.

Back at the house, I take tea with Magumi, a Japanese artist living there. She takes me to a dimly lit back room with one wall open to the courtyard to show me a sculpture she has been working on. It is taller than me, almost to the ceiling: a coil of plaited newspapers turned into rope, the kind of thick, seafaring cable I've seen at the docks. She does not tell me anything about the work—indeed, between

Japanese and broken Mandarin, we have few avenues for communication via words—but merely lifts the end of the coil to show me its frayed edges. I think of the Chinese-language newspapers at my grandparents' bungalow, stacked and aging. The memory of their smell has never left me. I think, distantly, I can smell them here. These papers are printed with human stories, with things that tie places and people far distant close together. Their binds are woven from heavy things. I glance into the coil and see the thinning newsprint wind around itself in a tangle. The tales have become tethers.

IN OCTOBER 1971, THE UNITED NATIONS PASSED
Resolution 2758. Taiwan—the Republic of China—
was expelled from the United Nations; the People's
Republic of China took its place.

Gong wrote little of the decades when he worked
as an instructor at Gangshan and then as a director
of political warfare at Hsinchu Air Base, serving as
counsel to young pilots who were flying surveillance
missions over China with the support of the CIA.
I tried and failed to gain more information, learning only that his military records remained closed. I
wrote to the base at Hsinchu and was told, succinctly,
that they remained grateful for his service. I worried,
wanting to know my family's role in a regime that
meant everything to those who sought to return to
the mainland; a regime that exercised incalculable

brutality against those it deemed a threat. But I could not know more than he had put to the page, and knowing what I did of the complex workings of the Cold War and of the martial law period in Taiwan, I came to realize that I might never account for those years of his life.

But I knew how his story ended.

Before the world shifted, a number of my grandfather's friends and colleagues had left for the United States and Canada, finding better working conditions on the crews of commercial airlines. Forced into early retirement, Gong had been out of flight for a handful of years. He had tried his hand as a salesman—not among his skills. He was miserable.

On the advice of those who had gone before, he applied to move the family—Po, my mother, and him—to Canada. In Canada, he could fly again, taking up a post with a commercial crew. In Canada, he would not be confined to the house, in a country to which he devoted his life, in a place he felt forgotten.

They moved in 1974, when Gong was fifty-five.

On arrival in Canada, the recruiters explained the process he would need to undergo. It was a surprise: coming from Taiwan, a country no longer recognized by the world, his credentials and citizenship would not carry over. He would not be given immediate clearance to fly. Gong asked how long it would take. Five years, they replied.

In five years, he would have been sixty. Too old to fly, the age restrictions ruled.

My mother and her parents found themselves in a new, cold country, speaking halting English, starting again.

With no experience beyond the air force and the government, my grandparents did what many immigrants do, taking whatever work was available to them. They became cleaners.

Throughout my childhood, I visited Gong on the industrial floor of that Niagara Falls canned-food factory. Did the strangers he met there know anything of his past? I watched him as he mopped, huddled and silent among the machinery, after the workers had gone home.

He rarely spoke to me of airplanes. For so long I could not imagine him in the sky, in flight.

LIN

n. FOREST; WOODS; GROVE

or

n. A GROUP OF LIKE PERSONS

In forests, new life is stitched into the ground.

12

THE LAST TIME I SAW MY GRANDFATHER, I WAS
twenty-one. He walked out onto the front porch of
the bungalow and stood leaning on the iron railing,
watching the street from the safety of the steps while
I loaded my bags from my short visit to Niagara Falls
into the car. Whether he had known me then, I cannot
say. He remained distant and quiet when I returned
to wrap my arms around him, holding him close. He
patted my back conclusively, as he often had, and said
simply, as if I were anyone in the world, "Bye-bye."

Some weeks later he returned to Taiwan—a decision made abruptly by my grandmother, alone—to
a veterans' care home in Kaohsiung. At eighty-nine,
quiet and fumbling, no longer able to speak English,
he needed support. It happened quickly, without time
for us to say goodbye. Po accompanied him on the

plane to Taiwan and then, relieved of his care, returned to Canada alone.

I imagined his new room many times: dark, with moonlight glazing the starched, institutional bedsheets, the door with a window to an empty hallway. I modeled it on every hospital room I'd ever seen. I tried my best to place Gong in that room but could see only the moment when he'd hugged me—now a stranger to him—on the bungalow porch. The picture of him alone in that room in Taiwan, abandoned, left a tightness in my heart that I couldn't endure.

My grandmother spoke as if he had already died.

I wondered what he thought during the flight back. Did he know he was going to Taiwan? Did he know the island that had drawn him back once more? I do not know if he remembered his past or its places.

Edward Said wrote that the pathos of exile is the impossibility of return. He wrote of those exiled by their governments, those who lost nations and topographies. Whatever the circumstances, there exists tragedy in being forced from home. Homes can continue to exist in so many material ways, but a life forged in its absence, on the move, is something different. Alzheimer's brings another exile: from the imagined world of past and memory.

There is an old Chinese tale, the myth of Kuafu,

which tells the story of a god who chased the sun. It is a tale told both to chastise the overambitious and to praise men's ambitions. It also contains, I think, a kernel of the sadness of exile. Kuafu, wishing to know what becomes of the sun when it reaches the horizon, walks ever westward. Exhausted and dehydrated, he dies a great distance from his home. What loss of dignity is contained in dying so?

But in Kuafu's story, there is a new beginning: His body decays, but his walking stick sends new shoots into the ground. It grows into an entire forest.

When my mother and I were in Taiwan we visited Kaohsiung, where Gong died. The city felt as if it existed as a reminder that we weren't there and that we should have been; our visit was an act of penance. To find his remains, my mother had written to the care home. We took a taxi past banana fields, past plastic-wrapped dragon fruits still on their trees, clutching the address of the temple on a scrawled note. A map masquerading as scrap paper. The temple's stairwell echoed as we ascended, up, up, until we alighted in a room of blue-doored niches decorated with air force wings. We had been given a key: a dingy, plastic thing on a heavy chain.

Gong's niche was on a row just one higher than the floor, so we had to sit on the concrete to greet him at eye level. We had never seen the photograph stuck to his urn, taken at the care home before his death. He looked far thinner than I had ever seen him, sallow, his cheekbones showing through his still-smooth skin. I closed my eyes, picturing that day on the porch; I didn't want to remember him any other way.

My mother held a clamshell, purple in her palm. She had carried it from the strait, from the beach in Hengchun where she had played as a child, and here, far inland from that shore, she left that piece of the sea with him.

•

IN THE DAYS AFTER, LIGHTENED, LESS BUR-dened somehow, Mom and I spent our time retracing her past life. She took me to her college and her school, to Yangmingshan, to the northern mountains and forests that she and Gong had loved. We stood in the narrow laneway outside the tiny apartment in Daan that she'd shared for most of her childhood with my grandmother, while Gong lived on the air bases at Gangshan, Chiayi, and Hsinchu. The concrete building sat blankly, bulging with the cubic protrusions of air conditioners. The third-floor windows were open just a crack, and I tried to picture who lived there now, if in that apartment was the scene I had once imagined, dusty and green. It had been a quiet street on the edge of the developing city when my mother was young, where fields had been not long before; now it sat in a central shopping district, lined with designer boutiques and coffee shops.

It rained ceaselessly. Escaping the cold, we ate at a neighborhood soup restaurant with plastic stools so low I thought they must have been made for children. On the table in the corner were two bowls of chili oil—one labeled with a warning. "Very spicy," it read. My mother and I filled our bowls. We each took a single mouthful before catching the other's gaze, wide-eyed, in pain. It was a game Mom played her entire life; a game we played together.

She'd told me stories of her childhood, of days when the base at Gangshan was perpetually sun-drenched, with the wide stretches of concrete and the buildings blazing white-hot in the afternoon light. She would spend her time in Gong's office, playing card games, trying to resist the urge to get into trouble. She had a habit for mischief; her longing for trouble wrestled with the demand for quiet discipline and meekness. Those afternoons were a relief. Po was busy with work in Taipei, and when my mother was there she was buffeted by Po's moods, like a boat in the wind. The air base was a world enclosed—hers and Gong's—and she took delight in spending her days lolling about, waiting for him to finish work.

On quieter days, the airmen who worked with Gong would take my mother fishing, dropping their lines with her in the small pond on the base's edge. My mother caught tadpoles, squelching through the shallows in search of frogs, turtles, and pond loaches, returning muddy to the tidy office Gong kept.

My grandfather always kept plants wherever he went, and he passed his love and skillfulness on to my mother and to me. Among the plants in his office was a hot pepper plant. When she first told me the story of the peppers I was nine, and we'd been sitting at a table nibbling hot peppers, testing our tolerance for habaneros. Her stamina in the face of searing heat fascinated me. If it was possible to train this skill, I wanted it, so I nibbled at the yellow, lantern-shaped fruit until I no longer felt any sensation in my tongue. She'd always had a taste for spice—Gong's time in Sichuan had instilled a love for cooking spicy food. When she found herself alone in his office, she told me, she had taken to plucking the peppers from their plant with her fingernails—which he had expressly told her not to do—licking her fingers, and leaving the stems intact. Her hands would swell and flush with heat, her lips would turn scarlet, and, of course, Gong would know what she had done. He never punished her, though—she laughed—because swollen, burning hands were punishment enough.

On those low stools, we forced our way through the bowls of soup, in pain but laughing, talking about Gong and about how Canada had made us soft, different. I stitched the three stories together in my mind: Mom with the pepper plant, the bowl of habaneros, and us, burnt-lipped on a rainy Taipei evening.

•

A FEW WEEKS AFTER LEAVING TAINAN, I'M journeying south again for a day, hoping to spend some time exploring the trails around Kaohsiung. My heart leaps at the thought of being in the southern warmth once again, but I'm quickly met with the curious feeling that I've never been to Kaohsiung without visiting my grandfather's remains. The city is a place that I've given over to him. In part, I feel as if it is a violation, a disrespect. But I know, too, that I have been holding my memory of him still for years when it ought to be moving. I comfort myself on the train journey from Taipei, watching for the things I know: a banana plantation, the clutch of high-rises at Taichung, the flat plateau of Tiezhen Shan (Iron Anvil Mountain). I turn my attention to the flat fields that line the rails on the journey out of the foothills and into the heat.

Shoushan (Monkey Mountain) sits west of Kaohsiung, shielding its northern quarters from the sea. The mountain rises above the harbor, formed from limestone crags like those in Hengchun, and scattered with the chalky forms of stalactites. It rests beneath a heavy blanket of secondary forest, banyans and sugar palms eking out an existence in the shallow soil. Their aerial roots creep over the coral, and rocky mounds conceal caves that house freshwater crabs, which occasionally skitter out near the path, delicate and pale.

The trail itself is easy, grading slowly to its flat peak, but Kaohsiung's heat differs so much from the cold in Taipei. It is midday by the time I near the top, panting with the humidity. The sun shines dully in the haze. From Shoushan's height, I can just about see across the city. I can pick out the hotel where I've stayed with my mother in the past and the patchwork of lanes I've come to know well. But I cannot see any farther, cannot see through the thickened afternoon air that rests a low crown on the city. I cannot see where I know Gong rests in a silent temple hall beyond the southern orchard fields, a short drive inland.

I do not visit him today. Instead I stretch his memory across Kaohsiung's haze, the city thrumming with heat. I watch the sky as a gull skips overhead, descending toward the harbor. My breath steadies. The seabird fades over the gray of the strait. The curl of a salt breeze slips between my limbs, and my body feels lighter as I turn and walk onward.

13

IN 1969, TAIWAN'S NATIONAL SCIENCE COUNCIL and the U.S.A.'s National Science Foundation agreed to the joint publication of the first comprehensive, contemporary flora of Taiwan. In the years that followed, they formed an editorial body, charged with the task of compiling the text. The six-volume *Flora of Taiwan* appeared in 1975—some sixty years after Bunzo Hayata attempted to document the island's botanical wealth in totality—and spanned more than five thousand pages. The first volume opens with a black-and-white photograph of the editorial committee, five lean men in suits, quietly smiling. One from the University of Pennsylvania, three from the National Taiwan University, and another from the New York Botanical Garden.

Once the civil war had ended and it appeared that

Taiwan was not a temporary stop-off for the mainland Nationalists, the building of infrastructure and boosting of the economy became key priorities. In parallel, scientific research blossomed once more. *Taiwania*, the island's journal of plant science, was launched in 1947 but published only a scattered number of volumes until the 1960s, when it began to publish extensively and in earnest. There was a pressure to view the island's nature as a resource: one article noted the need for plant science to serve economic development, listing a variety of plants, methods for their identification, and their uses. In a sense this was not new—indeed, much of the botanical research in the Japanese period served the needs of the forestry industry—but was formalized, reflecting the rapid development of the island. This increase in biological research eventually led, in the late 1970s, to the island's conservation movement. An updated second edition of *Flora of Taiwan* was published in the 1990s. And in 2008, scientists finalized the nation's first vegetation inventory.

I think often that it is in plants that Taiwan's recent history can readily be seen. Plants make visible so much of what humans have sought: in how they grow and thrive, how they mix in a wooded glade, in which species planted for our uses intermingle with those that have grown up quite spontaneously in home soil. Many of the island's botanical research centers were opened by the Japanese: the forest at Kenting was used as a forestry research center in the late nineteenth century and contains a wealth of introduced tropical species, while Taipei's Botanical Garden opened in 1896.

Plants come to represent us on city streets, in parks, in our poetry, and in shared dreams. Nature unfolds amid our worlds, shaped by our commitments—whether scientific, cultural, or political.

Botanical texts can teach us just as much. Historic floras interest me in part because lists of old plants and their semblance of order reveal a continuity between past scientific cultures and our present understandings of nature. Meaning is held in who named a species and how they came across it. The existence of historical specimens or their entries in a flora enables scientists to track which species appeared where and when. Looking backward, these samples allow us to understand transformations in how we manage the land, and how nonhuman nature, in turn, replies. Breakages appear too: plants that can no longer be found; plants that have been rehoused under the new genetic parameters in the Angiosperm Phylogeny Group, which orders flowering plants through DNA;

plant names that have shapeshifted so that I can only retrace their steps through online indices of plant names, searching for an etymology of nature. Plant histories—like human ones—have gaps in their genealogies.

I read old papers from *Taiwania*, scanning for titles that catch my interest, and revel in the places and species I know. Species of *Polytrichum* moss found on Qixing Mountain, mosses found submerged in ice water on Nenggao Mountain. I might never see these species myself, but in the careful words of botanical description I find ways to picture their ideal forms: lanceolate leaves, measurements in millimeters, serrate margins, and cells I would not see save for a microscope. I imagine, too, the journeys ventured to take those samples: botanists hauling packs and specimens over the same steep trailways I know, and with them I feel closer to something I cannot articulate. I search books and plant keys for something much greater than the specificity of specimens collected and pressed to a page.

On the southern Hengchun Peninsula, by the pools at Qikong Waterfall, there stood a *Barringtonia asiatica* fifteen feet high, alone on the edge of a lane. The tree's long leaves hung glossy green, a mere background to their flowers: white, puckered clusters of petals opening to a brush of fine filaments. They looked, I thought, like those fiber-optic lamps made from fishing line, with great feathered clusters of pink strands, yellow at their tips, and so lightly fused to the base of the flowers that the slightest disturbance showered the ground in a floral rain. I didn't know what the tree was at first, but I looked it up.

The fruit of the *Barringtonia*—known also as the "fish poison tree" or "box fruit tree"—hung heavy among the flowers, pale green cubic things the size of a fist, close to the branches. The species is listed variously as introduced and native to Taiwan, its status muddied. Like coconuts, the fruit is dispersed by water: floating by sea until tides bring it ashore in some distant place. And so this migrant tree has spread, from India through Oceania to the South Pacific. Afloat, its fruit can survive for longer than a decade awaiting landfall.

In Chinese, the *Barringtonia*'s name, 玉蕊科, means "jade stamen tree," but its pronunciation, yuruike, is what brought me joy: privately, I began to call it the eureka tree. A tree ever in search of newness, it makes a home wherever the sea might send it.

•

IT IS A GRAY WEDNESDAY IN TAIPEI WHEN Charlene and I venture toward the river intent on a walk. I have spent many days in the forests and long only for the flat span of the city. I ache from movement, and my knees are still knotted from the mountains. The waterside trail runs flat for a long distance, bordered only by the grasslands that cover the scrappy edges of Songshan Airport. Concrete covers everything else, from the riverbanks to the pavilions that sit between the streets and water.

So often Taipei has a kind of quiet to it: my body becomes anonymous amid innumerable others. I cannot stop to name the people any more than I could identify each tree in an overgrown wood, so I move swiftly, unnamed and unnaming. But here, the river flows slowly, where the low-rises cease their advance across town, and where the thickets of crowds disperse. The occasional cyclist or walker passes us. We greet strangers with a nod, as one does in the countryside, and stop only to notice the rare things that grow up amid the grasses, alone.

The Taiwan Basin is cut through with rivers. The Tamsui River, fed by three tributaries, runs into the city from the foothills in the south and east, a confluence flowing toward the strait. The Keelung River, which flows from the northeast, moves at an ambling pace, and we follow it seaward. We trace our course through where the land feels sunken down, bordered by mountains on the northern horizon, where I know we walk the edge of a single geological fault. As we round a bend, we pass a cluster of old fishermen spread out on chipped plastic stools, their lines bobbing in the shallows. They have come for the day: a Thermos sits on the ground next to them, as well as a plastic bag of fresh fruit. We offer them a quiet nod as we pass, and they return it. Quite what they might catch in the city, I'm not sure; the river is in a sorry state. A short distance past the fishermen, a shallow pool surrounded by reed grass seems a scenic improvement on the concrete banks, but a dead fish and what looks like the remains of a dog sway with the water. When we swam in the waterfall upstream at Huiyao, I didn't imagine the river flowing out to this.

We walk onward, past a park Charlene has never seen before, and she begins to tell me of the city's changes.

"I remember when Taipei 101 and that whole area was built, when the MRT lines were built. There's a station right outside my house. The construction took forever. It's all so new," she says.

I laugh, thinking that my mother has told me much the same. She remains confused by the network of trains and tall buildings overlaying the city she knew. I try to envision that scale of change. An app on my phone lays historic maps and aerial photos over Google Maps, and I do this often, wishing to see things as my mother did. In 1958, a field lay where her house would one day stand. A grainy photograph from 1974, the year she left, shows me the rooftop of her home, clustered amid the lanes and tenements that grew like a game of Tetris, spontaneous and erratic in shape. Taipei rose from low Japanese-style buildings with tiled roofs, to be replaced by apartment blocks, and then glassy office towers.

"My mom once told me a story," I say, "about taking her pet turtle for a walk at the city's edge. She tied a string around its neck as a leash, and when some neighborhood kids invited her to play, she tied the string to a rice plant. She never found the turtle again." I laugh at the thought of the turtle on a leash, then recover. "Mostly I just wonder how Taipei was so rural then."

I've watched my mother move unsteadily here, despite her knowing the language and in some deep-rooted way knowing the culture. I've navigated for her, moving between map and world, while she has searched for a trace of recognition. When she told me about restaurants she once knew, I would find them online and lead her to them. I worried, always, that she would get lost in her home country. But I have thought, too, of that day I watched her on the shore, beachcombing. Place-memories, however precarious, work their way into the body.

Like mine, Charlene's family came from the mainland. Born not long after my mother left for Canada, Charlene grew up as Taiwan changed.

"I grew up while people fought for democracy," she tells me, "when the censorship was really strict. I remember in the eighties my friend ordered an *Encyclopaedia Britannica* from overseas. And when we unwrapped it, the entry on China had the Chinese flag blacked out, all perfect, with a square glued over the top. There was just a blank in the middle of the page."

I nod, unsurprised. At sixteen, I'd asked for a copy of *The Communist Manifesto*, and despite having lived for many decades in Canada, my mother couldn't believe it was a book we were allowed to buy. I read that under martial law book bans in Taiwan extended not just to Marx but to authors whose names sounded similar: Mark Twain, Max Weber. My father told me once that when he had traveled to Taipei carrying a fax machine—a new technology back then—which he had needed for work, it had been confiscated; the authorities said it was a tool for espionage.

"During the Olympics, when the Chinese team was on screen, the flag was always blurred out. I didn't see that flag until I moved to the U.S. to go to college!" Charlene laughs.

Despite what she tells me, I feel a kernel of something: envy, perhaps, however misplaced. "You were here in all the decades my family wasn't," I say softly, and then immediately feel ashamed.

We reach a bend in the river. The Keelung is more beautiful here, open and free-flowing. A group of kayakers make their way upstream, their red helmets bobbing like buoys over the horizon.

I turn to the grasses, clasping a spike between my fingers. I repeat a rhyme I learned when studying botany, a small thing I have to offer: "Sedges have edges, rushes are round, grasses are hollow right down to the ground." I pluck a stalk as Charlene repeats the rhyme, and then we examine the grass, peering into its hollow center. Words made in another place feel strangely false here, ill-fitting, like a stretched-out knit. But still, I find comfort in knowing them.

Charlene and I walk farther, following the curve of the river westward past Songshan Airport. At an open field just beyond the runway, the rush of a landing plane reverberates overhead, tearing into the silence of the riverside. I stop short, having never been this close to the runway, and the memory it brings up is not mine. It is taken from the letter, and I have read it repeatedly in the last few days, as if in reading I might polish it like a stone. I've turned it over in my mind for weeks. I hold the words for a moment in my mind before speaking.

ONCE, I FLEW WITH THE AIR
Force Academy's principal to Taipei
for a meeting. The temperature was
bad, so we flew above the clouds. As
we reached the city, Songshan Airport
was closed due to the heavy fog. But
it was an important meeting, so I decided to land. Songshan was familiar
to me from my old days; I knew it better than my own hand, knew where the
small river curved around it. Above the
river, there was no fog, and following
it, I could make my landing.

After we landed, the control tower
messaged to ask where we were; they
could not see a thing. I replied, "We are
parked on the runway." The principal

leaned forward and gave me four words: "Riding clouds, driving fog." When the ground crew arrived, they said they'd known it had to be me, that only I could have landed in that fog.

These old men's praises made me sad.

I ONCE STOOD ON THE OBSERVATION DECK OF Taipei 101, scanning the horizon. My gaze came to rest on that runway—graying beneath the hills, wrapped by the river—where planes cut a parallel course across the city skyline. I could just about imagine him there.

The letter spanned twenty pages but never concluded. There was no signature, no cohesive ending. The final pages spiraled, paragraphs coiling back into the preceding story, ending mid-sentence. The letter was a map of his mind then, a labyrinthine thing of memory. Geographies blurred. Time shrank and receded in its pages, only to emerge once more, disjointed. I wondered if, in his illness, time had layered. Perhaps it flattened and folded into a single, multitudinous moment, the same way I carried words and places in my mind at once, multilingual and moving.

Reading, I felt at times in the spray of its branches—rows of characters overgrown in the wildness of his script—longing to emerge into a clearing. But his confusion thickened. And then, abruptly, it ceased.

When a storm releases a burst of air—a column known as a microburst—the rapid descent of the wind reaches the ground with the force of a tornado. On impact, it curls outward, its outflow changing direction, roiling the air through which it erupts. It spreads the way water from a tap turned on too quickly hits the sink, flooding outward and then up into the sky. Though it is merely wind, the force of the microburst can be deadly.

It was through such a storm that my grandfather took his last flight during a routine patrol over the Taiwan Strait. It was 1969. The technology to detect microbursts would not exist for another twenty years.

He never spoke of it and mentioned it without detail in his letter. I learned of the accident instead through my mother's memory.

Flying the coast, the sudden gust—the microburst—thrust his plane down. It fell rapidly, but the landing was braced by sand. He was lucky to crash on the beach not far from the Hsinchu Air Base. Had he been at sea, my mother said, he would likely have died.

My grandfather emerged from the plane entire, walking, and was rushed back to the base. In shock and never wanting to make a nuisance of himself, he insisted he was fine. He was a colonel in a senior role; perhaps no one thought to question him. Just hours later he drove himself to Taipei for a meeting. On arrival, he collapsed. Several vertebrae had been damaged in the crash and would cause him pain for the rest of his life.

He never flew again.

In the old myths of the sky ladder the heavens were reached by scaling a mountain or climbing a tree. Matsu reached heaven by climbing to a height and swaddling herself in fog. From such heights was the world held in order: our human realm beneath a vast, unreachable sky.

I think often of what Gong might have seen racing toward that vault of white. Tumbling into the coastal wind, did he see the ground as it rose up to greet him?

14

I PRINT OUT A MAP IN FULL COLOR, COUNTING each of the active fault lines with the tip of my finger. Forty-three in total, most of them cracked into the space of the narrow flatlands. They have names I've come to know: the Sanchiao and Chinshan Faults, which run across the north, past Taipei. The Chukuo Fault, inland from Tainan and Chiayi, where the Eurasian and Philippine Sea Plates meet. The Chelungpu Fault, where in 1999 the surface ruptured so violently that the fault line remains visible today, the ground excavated for public viewing.

I check my earthquake app. There have been only a handful in recent weeks, small ones, but more will come. Some researchers say they come in hundred-year cycles, arriving in a cluster of violent quakes and their aftershocks once each century. Their detractors point out that since the data spans little more than a hundred years, it could be impossible to know. But the island, some believe, is overdue for a bad earthquake. Like hurricane watchers, they await "the big one." There are predictions hoping to lend clarity to the opaqueness of future devastation. For now they tremble subtly, unnoticed beneath the ground. I mark their locations on my map and read websites on what to do in an emergency. *If indoors, stay there. If in bed, stay there. If outdoors, stay in the open.*

The records we keep of earthquakes depend upon our abilities to measure them. The nineteenth-century Gray-Milne seismometers in Taipei, Tainan, Keelung, Taichung, and Hengchun were followed by Japanese-made Omori types, and then the enormous Wiechert devices dampened with springs. A disastrous quake in Taichung and Hsinchu in 1935 prompted the creation of even more earthquake monitoring stations, such that Taiwan's network spanned sixteen locations by the end of the Second World War. With U.S. support, new instruments came into use through the 1950s and '60s. By 1973, the groundwork for an advanced detection system capable of recording magnitudes as low as 1 was put in place.

Taiwan now has one of the world's most advanced earthquake monitoring networks—with an early warning system designed to give notice to trains, hospitals, gas pipelines, and elevators—stretched over seventy-one locations. Its scope is broad: standard seismometers positioned throughout the country, accelerometers to measure seismic waves in differing geologic conditions, seismometers plunged into deep wells beneath the ground, sensors and cables installed in buildings, GPS observation, groundwater observation wells, and air-pressure gauges. The Central Weather Bureau collates the Earth's movements, and its website lists dozens a month. When an earthquake swarm—a cluster of quakes over a short period of time—arrives, the online list grows into the hundreds.

But we do not yet know how to predict earthquakes; we search for clues across science and folklore. Water in wells changes levels before and during quakes, so hydrographs are used. There are other more ethereal and less understood phenomena. In Haicheng, China, in 1975, it is said that in the days leading up to a 7.3 magnitude earthquake, the city's animals began to behave erratically. The city was evacuated, a decision that prevented massive loss of life. Some say that earthworms leave the soil in the moments before a quake, while according to Japanese legend catfish flee their ponds. In other places, strange cloud formations and lights in the sky have been observed before a quake: luminous glows that conspiracy theorists have called UFOs. But the glut of evidence for such strange sightings in recent years—thanks in part to the ubiquity of camera phones—has led to more scientific attention. There are those who believe these strange "earthquake lights" are just a burst of electricity working its way through stressed mineral structures or are like the triboluminescent flash produced when an object is cracked or broken, when the earth creates light like a peppermint snapped in a darkened room. The tales go back centuries, to ancient times, woven into myths and science. But regardless of our explanations, the temblors come.

I have found a strange quietude in following these attempts to chart nature: through maps, through flora, through seismicity. They give me something tangible to keep track of, not because a map can be equated with its territory but because it gives me some way of ordering the world and its complications. I once saw my grandfather write out words from an English dictionary, using each one in a sentence. Perhaps they gave him access to a world different from his own. When I walk a trail and feel foreign, I can name a tree or a rock. A map of fault lines, I think, might enable us to watch for things slipping away.

•

"I SAID GOODBYE MY FAMILY," PO CROAKED TO me once, dropping words the way she often did. I didn't ask anything more, realizing as young kids do that there are some sentences that do not ask for a reply.

She told us the past carefully, through stories de-limited and composed. But my sister and I had trusted the boundaries of our Chinese lives, as if that entire aspect of our history was concentrated in one place and in this single relation of grandparents to grand-children. The Niagara Falls bungalow was an island unto itself. It was the only place we spoke Mandarin; they were the people with whom we explored that side of ourselves. The neighborhood around their house was a suburban sea; we rarely wandered beyond the chain-link fence that lined the driveway, except to pick peaches from the neighbor's yard. If we saw the surrounding area, it was from the plush comfort of the Oldsmobile. Once in a while, we'd take the car on day trips over the U.S. border, stopping at Topps supermarket in Buffalo for loganberry juice and at Ponderosa for the all-you-can-eat buffet.

The bungalow was a place I loved: I spent long hours preparing food with Gong, rolling and folding jiaozi, and wasted mornings lying on my tummy on the orange shag rug in front of the television. As a child, I had Po's palate, a love of salt and sugar that meant we would slice and eat cold salted butter when no one else was around and then sprinkle white sugar on thin Chinese pancakes, rolled up and devoured in a mouthful. In the afternoons we ate Häagen-Dazs coffee ice cream with cornflakes.

My grandmother hid from view the past she didn't want us to know. I see it now, as if its traces had existed amid the old newspapers and soap-opera videos she'd fall asleep to in the basement.

My mother dialed two of the numbers on the old phone bill. One to China—her newfound cousin, Dong-ping—and one to Taiwan. When the call to Taiwan connected, my mother asked the stranger on the line if she had known my grandmother. "Chi-chien?" the voice replied, saying my mother's name. "Is that you?"

Months later, standing before us in the lobby of the Taipei Sheraton, Jing-xien wore a plaid coat, thick and quilted against the cold. Her shoes, I noticed, were as small as my mother's. She stood a good foot shorter than me, with cropped and graying soft hair. Across the table, over cups of tea, I watched her expressions: the wrinkle of her eyes, the intentness of her face while listening. Once in a while she would smile and nod, gracious and kind. In her seventies, she looked, I thought, uncannily like my grandmother.

On our way over, we had fretted over what to call Jing-xien, my grandmother's cousin. The complications of kinship were a tangle with which we were unacquainted. Every family member, depending on whether they are on the mother's or father's side, has a different title in Chinese. Having only ever known our grandparents, my sister and I never learned those names. My mother didn't know either: when I asked, she shrugged, unsure. Like so many children after 1949, she'd grown up without extended family. I searched the internet for names and found a table of titles for extended family, but there was nothing for a maternal elder cousin twice removed. This was a language none of us spoke. My mother decided that it was simplest if we just called Jing-xien auntie: Ayi.

Ayi lived near Daan Forest Park, a short distance from where my mother had grown up. She had left China as a small child and, like my mother, grown up in Taiwan, her own parents living in a military village like the one Po and Gong had lived in at Gangshan. She was only a decade older than my mother.

Unpacking a large envelope from her handbag, Ayi passed me an old photograph. In it, a much younger Jing-xien sat in the corner of a sofa wearing an oversized Christmas jumper. A three-year-old in turquoise overalls sat beaming next to her. Me.

I held the photograph for a minute, absorbing every detail. The jade-inlaid screen stood behind and the black leather sofa gleamed in the flash. It had been taken in the Niagara Falls bungalow.

Tears welled in my eyes, but I suppressed them, swallowing hard, not wanting to cry in front of someone new to us. But I had the evidence in my hand. I—we—had known her.

At the table, Mom and Ayi perused the menu, names for foods lubricating the slight awkwardness of this decades-stalled meeting. A plate of fried tofu appeared, followed by snow fungus speckled with wolfberry and lotus seeds. I could hardly eat, wanting only to focus on understanding the conversation between Ayi and my mother, their quiet revelations being laid out across the table. I turned to my tea, waiting for my mother's pauses for translation.

"Jing-xien says that she was always close with Gong. They used to play cards," my mother explained. "But she didn't always get along with Po."

In the late 1980s, Ayi and her family came over to Canada, staying for a few weeks in Niagara Falls. It was then that the photograph had been taken. A

few others from the same roll of film offered a time-
line of their visit: a stop at my father's office, a trip
to McDonald's, Happy Meals unboxed and spread
across the plastic table. In one photograph, my sister,
Ayi, and I sit close, smiling.

Something trivial but powerful had passed between her and my grandmother—she still did not
know what. But in the years after, Po never spoke
Jing-xien's name to us; her existence was covered over
as to be invisible.

Beneath the table, Ayi clasped my mother's hand,
holding her with tearful eyes. She said something in
Mandarin, too quickly for me to understand. I turned
to my mother.

"She says that she remembers when I was born,"
Mom translated. "In Kaohsiung. I lived with her until
I was three, while Po worked in Taipei."

I had never heard of these years my mother spent
apart from her parents, had always believed she had
been born in Taipei. My brow furrowed, and Mom
shrugged her shoulders in reply. She did not know
either.

I felt troubled. My mother had known Jing-xien in
her childhood, but had said nothing of her to us. That,
I could not account for. I wondered why she hadn't
sought Jing-xien out in the decades that had passed. I

turned to her, searching, but found in her face a grief I had not seen before. She held her breath a moment, her eyes creased with tears. I saw her gathering her strength. My mother's world had been as bounded as my own. How could she, alone, have strayed from the limits Po had set?

Midway through the meal, while my mother was in the restroom, Ayi leaned over to me and spoke for the first time in quiet, halting English.

"Your mom and daddy—" She broke off, gesturing separation by moving her hands apart. I nodded, not knowing how to tell her that my parents had divorced nearly twenty years ago, not wanting my mother to return in the midst of such an explanation. I did not know how to ask why we had all been kept apart. The years hung between us anyway, unspoken.

My sister and I had grown up not knowing of Ayi's existence. She had lived not knowing what became of my mother or of us.

In the weeks that followed, I went back over the recordings I'd made with Po, looking for a slip that indicated she had mentioned Jing-xien to us, just once. I searched Gong's letters, looking for her name: my grandfather had never said anything, and the letters, too, showed nothing. I looked for some evidence that it was I who had been mistaken. I had spent my life repeating the words of my mother, my grandmother: we had no other family. Were our memories so short?

The loss of my grandmother's family on the mainland, as abrupt as it was, was something Po had shared with us. We had mourned it, in what small ways we could. I had turned to that story for explanation so often—for her anger, for the distance she had kept between all of us—but could never find satisfaction in its reasons. The instincts I had to order and make sense of the past fell flat. I knew only that there were words she could not speak, explanations that dwelt only in the darkness between feeling and form. There exist losses impossible to distill into mere stories.

15

ON SEPTEMBER 21, 1999, SHORTLY BEFORE TWO in the morning, a magnitude 7.6 earthquake struck central Taiwan. The ground shook in the dark for over a minute, a violent convulsion that spread across the island from its epicenter in Chichi, north of the Choshui River. It felled cities as if they were forests, destroying or damaging a hundred thousand buildings, killing nearly two and a half thousand people, and injuring eleven thousand others. Jiu'er'yi ("921") was the deadliest earthquake the island had seen in more than sixty years.

Its traces linger even now. I come across them in old news reports, rehashed annually for the quake's anniversary; in geological studies; in the pages of guidebooks. Images of shredded concrete and folded roads, a crumpled temple, and an athletic track curled acrobatically in on itself. An elevated highway, blanketed by what was once a nearby slope. A fault line is preserved as a display. The quake triggered nearly twenty-six thousand landslides in central Taiwan. The drives I've taken through the western foothills show the bare scars where forests were shaken free of their hillside homes.

More than three hundred years ago, when the Qing official Yu Yonghe journeyed north in search of sulfur, he came to an "earthquake" lake, a bamboo forest flooded when a quake rent the earth. Yu had never seen such a thing and was struck by the magnitude of such change: How could it be possible for the land and the water to change places? In 1999, these transformations took place again; the Jiu'er'yi quake created at least three new lakes. One of them was formed by the flooding of the Shuiyang Forest.

水漾森林, Shuiyang Senlin (literally "Forest of Overflowed Water"), formed when a landslip blocked a stream of the Shigupan River in the foothills near Alishan, in central Taiwan. The forests at Alishan are famous for their scale: thousand-year-old cypresses and cedars blanket the remote hills. "God trees" spanning a house's width, they grow slowly, even by dendrological standards. On Jiu'er'yi, September 21, the stream flooded the cedar forest, forming a lake nearly a third of a mile in length. The lake is now scattered with the standing remains of the wood, ghosts in a still-living landscape.

•

STORM CLOUDS SEEM TO SPIRIT THEIR WAY through the walls. I wake before dawn and discover that I can see my breath, with mountain cold seeping through the wood panels of the room. Winter has moved in across the north and the mountains, casting everything green in a pale frost of damp condensation. The cockerels seem immune to both cold and darkness, crowing as the haze of night still hangs across the morning. I check the time; it isn't yet six.

I have gathered a group of hikers I met at Nenggao for a two-day trek through the cedars over occasionally steep terrain, seeking the Shuiyang Forest: Julie, a teacher in Taipei, and David and Alex, both engineers in Hsinchu. Tucked two to a bed, we sought a night of relative comfort, knowing that today will likely bring a winter storm. Not wanting to wake them, I shuffle out of bed and make my way to the bathroom, gently pulling the door shut behind me. The latch clicks, and I hear one of the others yawn through the door.

The basin is peeling and stained in one part; the mirror shows the dullest of reflections. Dark patches have gathered below my eyes. In the island's sun, my skin has grown peppered with faint age spots, an inheritance from my mother that she laments, but I am glad of. Wind has lent my cheeks a sting of constant color, giving the impression that I am perpetually flushed with embarrassment. I clean my teeth, tie my hair in a knot, and splash icy water onto my face, drying my skin on my sleeve. We sought basic accommodation for the night; the guesthouse in Xitou, just north of the trailhead in central Taiwan, is true to its word.

By the time I emerge, the others have begun to wake. Julie is rolling up her thick socks, while Alex and David shuffle slowly from their small bed. A beam of sunlight has broken through the hills, lighting gold on the gathered mist. I press my forehead to the window, breathing steam onto the pane, and notice that the remains of raindrops pattern the glass. It has rained overnight, and we will likely see more today.

There is a knock at the door, and a woman greets me with a breakfast tray. Simple fare—sliced white bread sandwiches with American cheese and hot soy milk—but we each relish the meal, sipping slowly from the steaming mugs as if to avoid setting foot outside, where the cold still lingers. The silence of morning conceals the slipping-away of time, so I down my soy milk in a gulp. To make it to the lake by sundown, we need to get going.

It is half an hour's drive to the trailhead, up a road that winds so tightly I have to train my gaze straight ahead, blocking the thought of my own carsickness from myself, lest the idea of nausea make me ill. It isn't helped by the fog, which grows heavier the higher we climb, leaving us unable to see more than a few feet in front of us. So early in the day, the roads are near empty, and we have only the reflective guide of the occasional barriers to keep us from the cliffs. We take each turn slowly, warping around the curves so that every turn drags, stretching the knots in my stomach. I distract myself by noting aloud every sign welcoming us to the Shanlinxi Forest: twelve signs, a cartoon for every animal of the Chinese zodiac, each one saying "Welcome! Hi!" By the time we reach the gates, I am almost accustomed to the churn in my gut. The others appear to have weathered the drive with remarkable resilience and arrive without a trace of sickened pallor.

We stop to buy cups of coffee—acrid but at least steaming hot—and guzzle them as we assemble our gear. The trailhead is a thirty-minute walk from the parking lot, just enough to warm us to our packs, and in those early moments the rain arrives, slowly at first, but with a wave of damp mist, enough to wet the skin. A twinge of worry crosses my mind; other hikers have canceled their trips to the mountains this weekend, due to snow on the forecast. We've been warned that this trail could be tricky in wet conditions. I raised the possibility of not going last night and was greeted with enthusiastic dismissal. But in relief, as we reach the trail, I see a jumble of footsteps patterning the mud ahead of us. We aren't the only ones here.

The journey begins on an old logging road that climbs steeply into the mountains from Shanlinxi. The trunks of red cypresses thicken as we walk farther, bracing ourselves with hiking poles against the slick mud. A tractor has been up recently; its toothed remnants remain, deep enough that rainwater has begun to pool in the imprints. After a time, though, the mud relents and the track turns to packed soil, narrowing to the width of a walker or two at most; it is evident by the size of the trail that logging here took place by hand and on foot.

It is a long walk, mostly spent focused on keeping moving, marking progress on the seven-hour journey to Shuiyang. We come up behind a group of hikers—at least fifteen people—huddled along a clearing on the track, and greet them as we pass. "Zao an, zao an," I repeat, receiving a chorus of hellos in reply.

The minutes drag as rain seeps from my wrists to my sleeves, and thin rivulets run from my hood to my neck. By late morning, my limbs have grown faint and weak despite the ease of the trail. The cold is sapping my energy. Stopping, I unpack a paper box of mushroom-and-cabbage baozi and fried turnip cakes—all delicious despite the cold—a small feast, eaten bobbing up and down to stay warm. In no more than five minutes we are pressing on into the thickets.

Wading into silver grass is akin to bathing in a sharpened pool of reeds, the fronds of seed holding fast to the rain. A wet slap is followed by the leaves, whetted as a blade, leaving paper cuts on the skin of our necks and hands. The grass rises above us, screening our view of the trail ahead, leaving us to traverse a patch just wide enough to set one foot in front of the other. I soon find myself lost in the task of swimming through them.

On approaching a hut, we meet the largest group on the trail, some twenty hikers in a row led by a cheerful woman in a neon windbreaker. We heard them before we saw them; their leader carries a small radio around her neck, perpetually blasting Mandarin pop music as the group shuffles along the narrow path. I am struck at first by the oddity of venturing along a mountain trail and not wanting to listen for the rustle of leaf, the chatter of birdsong, but the group gawks at silent us as we pass. The group's guide smiles at us, wishing us luck, and I sense among them a sense of play I do not have. The pop music they hike to is joined by laughter and ease. I think of the jollity in the word used to describe hikers in Mandarin: 山友 shan you ("mountain friends").

For many years, Taiwan's trails and permit system have been difficult for foreigners to navigate, with little trail information available in English, though this has changed somewhat in recent years. Once in a while, I have to translate the trail markers or signposts, picking out the words I know like "mountain," "forest," and "water." Put to use in navigation, the scope of my literacy grows with every hike. But non-Taiwanese hikers remain a minority in the mountains; my pink cheeks and curly hair mark me, too, as foreign.

A short distance ahead, we meet the gateway to the high forest. The rock face isn't quite perpendicular, but after the relative flatness of the trail so far, it presents a daunting prospect. Lined with fixed ropes dripping from the rain, it ascends perhaps a hundred feet in a scattering of rock and packed soil to a forested cliff edge above, where the trail continues. David launches ahead, spryly tackling the stony clefts without a hiking pole in order to ensure the rest of us make it up comfortably. Julie hangs back, and I see quickly that both Alex and I have been sandwiched in the middle as we are the less experienced hikers.

Somewhat discouraged, I begin the short climb, pushing myself upward with the force of my hiking stick, clasping the mucky ropes to prevent myself tipping backward with the weight of my pack. It is not terribly difficult, but it is steep, and in the mountains my legs appear to have discovered a fear of heights previously unknown to me. I felt the same nervous tremors on the landslides on the Nenggao Trail, a kernel of nauseating fear that seemed to overrun my usual recklessness. I think, as I clamber my way up, that perhaps it comes with age. My mother, with the same fear, has always stayed far from a trail's edge. I am nearing the top when I begin to think I cannot make it and make the mistake of glancing behind. The others have grown small on the ground below. Vertigo sways me.

"You're eighty percent there," I hear David call from above, so I turn my attention to the task of the final 20 percent, pulling myself over the final clefts of rock with the ropes until I find myself on the needle-carpeted path up above.

The ground higher up has the sponge lightness of evergreen forest, acidic, well drained, and littered with soft flakes of faded vermilion bark. Moss overflows from the darkened hollows, turning the world to a flattened, two-tone green and rust. Only in the breaks between trees can light enter, and even then it is merely a shaving, dulled in the fog that hangs in the gaps. The trees themselves seem impossibly tall; rows of thick cedar and cypress trunks array the hillsides, lined like soldiers for battle, reaching sturdy to the sky. The trees have the quietude of age, with no scrub amid them. The trail is an open nave, the forest empyrean in scale.

•

THE ENDANGERED TAIWANESE CYPRESSES— both the "red" and "yellow" *Chamaecyparis* native to the island, known as false cypresses to distinguish them from other cypresses in the family *Cupressaceae*— have long been prized for their wood, with resistant, thick-growing trunks and few branches. In the early twentieth century, the Japanese opened these mountains to forestry, logging the hills around Alishan and building a reputation for Taiwan's cedar and cypress forests: rich with long-lived trees, the forests for many decades served the demand for camphor timber for temple construction, carvings, and precious medicinal oils. In February 1912, the British naturalist and plant collector Henry John Elwes landed in Taiwan, intent on seeing the ancient cypress cloud forests that lay hidden in these mountains. He was accompanied by the botanist William Robert Price, who alongside adding specimens to the Herbarium at Kew, exchanged plants with Bunzo Hayata. To get to the mountains to collect plant samples and net butterflies, Elwes "found chairs carried by Chinese coolies, a most agreeable mode of travelling in the mountains." Those same locals, Elwes enthused, "took great interest in my work and retrieved birds in the jungle or climbed trees to gather plants." Foreign botany was made possible by local knowledge and labor.

He wrote of trees whose species he had seen rarely elsewhere, save the high peaks of Sikkim in the Himalaya. The trees needed many centuries and very specific conditions in which to grow, preferring cool and damp places as afforded by the high altitude and humidity that make Taiwan one of the few places suitable for them. The farther into the forest the botanists delved, the thicker the trees grew: camphor and mahogany, strewn with orchids, and eventually, near Alishan (called Arisan in Japanese), the cypresses.

Elwes found trees between five hundred and a thousand years old, growing perhaps only a foot every century. "It therefore seems probable," he wrote, "that these Cypresses may attain a greater age than any in the world except the *Sequoia gigantea* of California." Of the seven false cypress (*Chamaecyparis*) species that exist in the world—famously growing on the North American West Coast—two of them, the red and yellow, are Taiwanese. When Elwes visited, the forest held great spaces between the giants, with no seedling trees rising up through the bed of fine soil. But the trees, he found, were durable: He sent seeds on to England, where the cypresses and cedars, hardy enough to withstand the cold winter, grew unabated. In the years that followed, the samples gathered by collectors would form the basis of a strong gardeners' interest in Taiwanese species of cedar and cypress. These are now found in botanical gardens worldwide, though their range remains limited in the wild.

In a rare photograph from his expedition, Elwes sits beside a mammoth cedar tree—felled and planed for timber, its trunk at least thrice his burly width—in the swelling growth of the forest. He wrote that among the felled trees he counted those with upward of four hundred rings, more than eight feet in diameter. And he observed, too, the tensions between his

Japanese guides and the local Chinese and indigenous workers. Forestry was a key industry through and for which the mountains were mapped and administered, with many people pressed into work in the logging industry. Elwes's brief account of Taiwan in his *Memoirs of Travel, Sport, and Natural History* provides an insight into the botanical conquest of the island and the human communities that underpinned it.

After Taiwan passed back to Chinese hands, the export of cypress and cedar wood expanded rapidly, peaking in the 1970s. Much found a market in Japan, until growing environmental pressure resulted in greater regulation of the forestry industry. Efforts to pull the trees back from total extinction depended upon a change in perspective; the forests had, for nearly a century, been viewed as a resource for the rapidly developing nation. In 1991, following Taiwan's turn to democracy, the Forestry Act was passed, banning logging in natural forests. The trees have since become of vital tourism value, alongside the growing recognition of the role of forests in structurally strengthening the hillsides in the event of earthquakes and landslides. Were it not for the conjunction of activism and democracy, however, it is difficult to say how the forests might have fared.

These cypress and cedar forests have, since the ban,

become the stage for some of the world's most difficult conservation battles: posters in no fewer than five
languages appear on the trail, warning of the consequences for illegal logging. Yards-wide stumps of felled
trees dot the spaces between the trunks, mournful in
the low-hanging haze. Seeking the enormous payouts
of illegal logging—a few hours of work netting more
than the average monthly wage—the majority of tree
poachers arrive by night on the steep slopes that are
both difficult to reach and impossibly dark. Still, forest
rangers attempt to root out the poachers, employing
both tactical police forces and forensic methodology
in their work. The island is now building a DNA database of its trees, effectively creating a genetic footprint for samples of illegal wood, a forensic track to
the forest in which a tree was felled, in the hopes of
increasing successful prosecutions. The situation for
both poachers and police remains brutally dangerous: poaching groups are often armed, and many are
staffed by precarious migrant labor. The criminal networks that sustain the illegal industry from a distance
often view the poachers and their lives as disposable.
The trailside posters have a cartoon image of a rat in a
thief's mask, or 山老鼠 shan laoshu ("mountain rats"
being the nickname for tree poachers), a trivialization,
perhaps, of a very complicated form of wildlife crime.

THE TREES ARE SO TALL I CAN HARDLY SEE
their branches, their green foliage hanging in flat
sprays that droop ever so slightly near their crowns,
the way shaggy hair might drape around one's neck.
The greenery's sloping shape, held against the military
exactitude of the trunks, resembles to me the Chinese
character that builds forests: 木 mu (the wood radical).
Arboreal 木 spreads wide and tall. And like timber
set to work, 木 builds all the words around it: 樹 shu
("tree"), 林 lin ("grove, woods, or forest"), and 森林
senlin ("forest"), the multiplicity of tree shapes indi-
cating the scale of the woodland. 木 carries a vastness
of possibility, like the giants in these hills. And at
their scale, just two trees would make a forest.

The name of the Swedish botanist Carl Linné—
often dubbed the father of modern taxonomy—is
rendered in Chinese with the characters 林奈, pronounced "lin nai," meaning "someone related to the
forest" or "someone who endures the forest." It seems
a small satisfaction that, while in English we have tax-
onomized his name—calling him Carl Linnaeus—
the Chinese, instead, layered in his name a meaning
true to botany itself. I think of the wood radical in
my own name, 李, and the many that stand in my

grandmother's. I find a quiet ease in the notion that forests can be built into who we are.

It is a brutal descent toward the Shuiyang Senlin, taking us down the steeply graded height of the ridge where the forest mixes again, becomes broad-leaved and stony, and on into the valley below. We make our way slowly—the slope is still treacherous from the rain—clasping the fixed ropes that appear every so often to lower ourselves between rough-hewn footings a yard apart. It is painful work with my aching knees, every step singeing my joints, and I grow silent in frustration and exhaustion. We have hiked a long way, and the peace of the forest above was a solace. This final descent has caught us by surprise. After forty minutes of lumbering progress, the valley floor opens to the clearing of the forest lake.

Stark sunlight falls in the valley. The late-day light begins to catch the blasted whites of the trees, bared of bark in their watery home. The lake is reminiscent of the alder carrs I've seen back in Germany, streams winding their ways through forests that thrive in water. But here, the remnants of Taiwan cedar are an eldritch vision: they stand vacant with water scaling their trunks, wasted shards bleached in the sun, pointed and jagged at their tips.

One of the species found here, *Taiwania*

cryptomerioides, was named by Bunzo Hayata for the island and the genus, *Cryptomeria*, which literally means "hidden parts," in reference to their seed cones. He considered the tree his greatest botanical achievement, devoting multiple texts to the subject of the *Taiwania*. In time, the cedar came to be known as the "coffin tree" for its popularity in coffin making. I think, in seeing it up close, that the view at Shuiyang seems rather true to that name; the forest graveyard pulses with the magnetic, haunted energy of lost life, with the eerie quality of a horror film.

We set camp on the opposite shore of the lake, avoiding the stretch of gravel beach where a man has already set a makeshift camp to feed the incoming hiking groups, charging, I expect, a premium for the service. The far bank where we find ourselves is slightly more secluded, tucked onto a flat stretch of gravel that makes it difficult, but not impossible, to peg out our tents. Battered but satisfied, I settle down for a warm drink.

I pour out cups of tea for the four of us and then find a large rock by the shore on which I can sit alone. I sip in silence. The lake has settled to an early evening calm, every tree reflected in perfect mirror. I press my hands to the enamel of the mug, feeling for the first time since breakfast the glow of warmth. I steady myself, until I can hear only the movement of my breath, the occasional rush of wind on the canopied hills. A bird appears—dark-backed, crested, and yellow-bellied—flitting from the thickly treed slope toward the shore, pausing briefly near the trees on the gravelly edge of the lake, its tiny body glowing doubled in the water. This brief appearance stretches into a quiet eternity as I watch, noticing every small, flickering movement at the margin of the wood. And just as quickly, the yellow tit, one of Taiwan's rarest birds, is gone.

The sun glows golden on the tree backs, the green of the water magnified by the light. The other groups of hikers arrive, and I watch them cheering their successes and viewing the lake with curiosity. They gather on the opposite shore to take photographs, practicing poses in the lowering sun, as the sky turns to a streaked pink-blue, the shadows of trees dark against the rose incandescence of the half-light. The mirrored world extinguishes into darkness, and sleep calls. Our tents stand ready and warm.

But just before slipping into an exhausted slumber, I step out into the night. My breath catches in clouds amid the cold. I shuffle my hands together, seeking warmth in their friction, and turn my gaze upward. The sky is streaked with stars—bright dewdrops on a dark canopy—and I think perhaps this is the clearest sky I've ever seen. The otherworld of the earthquake lake is a blackened shroud, but the quarter-mooned sky stretches light forever.

•

THE MORNING BRINGS LITTLE WARMTH. I AM awake before five, while mist is still rising blue on the water, the sun not yet reaching us. The tents are wet with condensation, shaking drops onto us with each movement. My breath comes short in the cold air, puffing meager warmth with every exhalation. Despite being in a valley, we are still two thousand meters above sea level, and December on the island can be deceptively cold. I set to work on coffee and porridge, as much to warm my hands as to sharpen the senses.

Nourished and caffeinated—the brown sugar I sprinkled rather too liberally into the oats coursing through my blood—we begin to pack up, hoping to make it to the trail before the other groups, who haven't yet risen for breakfast. They are beginning to make noise, though—I can hear tents unzipping across the lake—and we don't want to be stuck behind a large group on the ascent toward the cypress trail. I take a moment to glance out over the mist-glazed sur-face of Shuiyang. It is far bluer than yesterday—the sediment has settled after the rain—and I can see a good way through its gleaming depths. A feeling rises that I can only describe as compulsion.

I turn to my friends—already shaking their heads in response to my unasked question—and kick off my boots. The hikers across the lake have begun to emerge from their tents, marveling at the blue haze between the trees. I work my way out of my clothes and into my suit, tentatively slipping into the scene, swimming silent into the silvered vale. I swim out to-ward the remnants of the cedars, their new growth of ferns skirting the break between water and air. The earthquake shook the forest to its end; but this lake is a new place, a new ecosystem, and it is grow-ing steadily. I watch the entirety of the scene turn to color. Green on the old trees, blue in the water, the blaze of sun rising warm overhead. The chatter of on-lookers fades to a muffle as I hear only my stroke on the surface, the quiet life in the lake.

By the time we hike out of the valley and up to the crest of the hillside above, the morning is fully formed and bright, a clear blue dome overhead sear-ing with a hot sun. We can see from this height what was shrouded by cloud yesterday: the ridge of high mountains to the east, and the shafts of the ghost trees in the lake below.

The cedars of this forest were once abundant. Fossils of them have been found as far away as Alaska, dating from more than 100 million years ago, and in Europe some 60 million years ago. Once spread throughout the Northern Hemisphere, these lonely trees now stand endangered in the few places they remain. They are dependent on disturbance for regeneration. Landslide and fire sustain the coffin trees, growing across these precarious slopes in their own time, spread by wind, by rockfall, by natural disaster.

Edward Said wrote of the human habit of romanticizing loss, the tendency to render and celebrate in literature the irrevocable gaps rent between peoples and the places from which they come. I turn to his words often, finding in their exactitude an articulation of my own feelings. Said wrote of the ways we aestheticize a lonely death. I think of the trees—once spread far but now diminishing. My grandfather died—skin on brittle bones—without us. His memory came undone, but the places he lost were not forgotten. They were written into him in ways he could not have known: in language, in body.

He wasted away once he could no longer eat, his heart failing in the night. Gong died alone, and it is for this aloneness that I have not forgiven myself. Nothing in this death could be called beautiful.

For so long I have treated Taiwan as a haunted place, guided by memories that are not mine. I've carried the weight of my grandfather's death into the landscape, guilt and grief intermingled. But his death and Po's have brought me new possibilities for knowing. Sadness has lightened, grown lean on my bones. I find in the cedar forest a place where the old trees can span all our stories, where three human generations seem small. The forest stands despite us.

Deep in the valley below, sunlight gleams on the bare bleach of the skeleton trunks, the water glazed as a mirror. It grew full-colored as I swam, like blood flushing the skin, and from here, I think, it seems even brighter. I wonder, looking out at the coffin trees, if there is not life in that lakeland forest.

16

THE NORTHERN RAIN COMES HEAVY IN WIN-
ter. Clouds hang wool-thick over the mountains
around Taipei. I greet the peaks each morning as I
leave the apartment, peering down Chengfu Road
toward the Four Beasts. Their damp green seems to
dissolve into sky, as if the rain comes from the trees
themselves. The hills show me something my grandfather might have known well, because what else is
flight if not a journey into cloud?

Qixing Mountain stands between the city and the
sea, in a small chain of mountains that clamber steeply
between the Tamsui River and the coast. Today, little
of it is visible in the fog and heavy rain. But there is a
sound, otherworldly and fierce, which is magnified by
the sulfuric stench that rises with it, a firestorm shriek
hissing into the air. I have never heard such a noise:

volcanic fumaroles boil at the base where groundwater is heated until steam erupts from small cracks in the stone.

Sulfur drew the Han Chinese to Taiwan in the seventeenth century, when Yu Yonghe had ventured his way to the north. At the tip of the island the ground was known to smoke (fumaroles take their name from the Latin word fumus, for smoke), lakes and streams known to boil. In the nineteenth century, when Robert Swinhoe wrote to the Royal Geographical Society of his travels on the island, he noted that the volcanic chasms near the sulfur mines "had everywhere a pale sickly tint of yellow and red . . . hot steam gushed in jets with great noise and force, like the steam from the escape-pipe of a high-pressure engine." Today, the slope looks like a gaping wound in the mountain. I come first to a small spring boiling at the trail's edge. Where the cracks leach sulfur, the rocks are tinged yellow-green, a color that strikes me as belonging not to nature but to a world deep in Earth's belly. The silver grass nearby blooms red instead of its usual white.

Qixing is part of the Datun Volcanic Group—a group of more than twenty volcanoes clustered north of Taipei—reaching eastward until Keelung. Some 2.8 million years ago, when the tectonic plates beneath Taiwan collided, eruptions began launching into the world. Lava oozed to andesite, cooled, went dormant. And then, eight hundred thousand years ago, the eruptions formed the small mountains of this northern mass: Qixing Mountain (literally, Seven Stars Mountain) is magmatic and multiple, eroded into seven peaks. Grass grows over the curving mounds, giving the entire region a softened look (the mountain was once named Caoshan, "Grass Mountain"). The eruptions stopped two hundred thousand years ago, but a volcanic underbelly remains: the magmatic chamber reaches eastward to the still-active volcano of Guishan Island, and scientists continue to speculate as to when the Datun volcanoes may erupt again.

Qixing Mountain's height makes it vulnerable to the weather that courses in from the sea; it sits braced against northern monsoons. On this slope, only silver grass and cane survive; on southern slopes, shielded from the cold and warmed by the geothermal activity beneath the soil, a few trees grow. As I make my way uphill, every so often I spot a lonely windblown tree and glance at its leaves to check: *Trochodendron aralioides*, the wheel tree or "cloud-leaf tree" (雲葉樹, yun ye shu), has evergreen leaves that radiate, almost a whorl. In summer, its inflorescences resemble spokes. The species was first recorded mostly in the isolated forests of the Central Mountains and photographed by William Robert Price, the botanist who traveled with Henry John Elwes in 1912. Normally found at altitudes between two thousand and three thousand meters, at Qixing they live as low as eight hundred meters.

The tree's botanical beginnings were unstable. The taxonomic science by which we ordered the tree shifted. First recorded in Japan, the tree was moved from family to family, until eventually the species was categorized in a new order: *Trochodendrales*, an order with two genera, both with just a single species. All of the tree's other relatives—found as fossils on distant continents—are extinct.

Do our shifting orders and genera mean anything to the cloud-leaf tree? The tree dwells ever in solitude, in the sea winds of these battered hills.

•

SOME MONTHS FROM NOW, MY MOTHER WILL board a plane to China, a far different country from the land my grandparents left. Will she see the home my grandmother grew up in and meet the family who lived in her absence? I wonder what remains of the old homestead—the square block with the chandlery and the soy bean factories, the bakery and the teahouse.

Will she see my grandfather's village in the north and sweep the graves of our ancestors?

I think of what my mother might say when Dong-ping greets her. Will she find in my mother's face something familiar?

I am leaving Taiwan soon, flying back to Berlin in the coming days. I feel the weight of the departure, a disjointed frustration at not being able to be in two places at once. I want to stay, but I have to return.

I have spent the past week in preparation. I visited my mother's old apartment, memorizing the façade, its window frames and weathered concrete. I went to Jing-xien Ayi's house for lunch and held her hand over a table laden with my Taiwanese favorites: braised eggs, marinated tofu skins, sticky rice dumplings, and cabbage. In the middle of our meal, she leaped out of her chair and came back with an enormous wooden cutting board, darkened with age.

"Ni Gong geile wo zhege." ("Your grandfather gave me this.") "Sixty years ago, when I was a girl," she added in English.

She has used the board for her entire life, rolling dough on its smooth surface, the way Gong used to when he made jiaozi or hezi. I reached out and touched the cool butter-brown wood, feeling in my fingertips the closeness to something he once held, wood that had so much of my family's life in it. I choked back the tears that flooded me then, not wanting to bring my grief to Jing-xien Ayí's kitchen table, and turned to my tea, hiding my emotion in its warmth.

After lunch, she walked me to the lift, hugging me close in goodbye. The doors slid open, and as I stepped in to depart she cried out clearly in English, "Merry Christmas!" The lift doors closed, and I pressed my-self against its mirrored wall, the wave of emotion I'd been suppressing overtaking me. I wept not from loss but from the knowledge that I'd gained family. But as I stepped into the street, my phone pinged with a message: a Snoopy sticker from Ayi, hearts flowing out from the black-and-white dog's cartoon form. I felt joy at her lighthearted affection as I made my way along Heping Road.

That evening, Charlene walked with me to Longshan Temple. We found it swathed in the half-light of the city, brightened only by the glow of the joss sticks in its halls. Shadows lingered in the cor-ners, a vision of the temple's past made possible by an unexpected power cut. In the absence of light, the tourists had left and the temple stood near empty.

Charlene led me through the process of bai bai, each clutching a single joss stick as we moved through the temple. At Matsu, in the rear hall, I felt a familiarity. I was able to think clearly. Po and Gong had been granted safe passage to the island, a home at sea. Taiwan gave us a place to return to. I held my breath a moment, hearing only the darkness, and then the electricity was restored. A golden light flooded through the halls, and a pumped stream swelled in the waterfall at the temple's gate. I left grateful for the moment of silence the darkness had offered.

•

QIXING MOUNTAIN BLEACHES MY SENSES. THE wind above the cane is so loud I cannot hear my thoughts. As I near the peak, I tuck my body low to the steps to avoid being blown back. Fog turns the world to white, and every inhalation I take has the cut of ice. The rain has thinned to erratic drops that every so often fall directly on my face. But it is no matter; I am soaked through, as much with rain as with cold sweat. I discover exhilaration in my discomfort.

The peak opens to an empty plateau, spread over with rocks and a small platform of wood. A pillar is carved with the altitude—1,120 meters. Beyond the slopes, somewhere beneath the volcanic heights on which I stand, is the city. On a clear day, Taipei can be seen from the height of Qixing, and so can the coast in the opposite direction. Now the storm is spread thickly against the sky. I can scarcely see the ground I've walked over, and I cannot see the lanes of the city or the swathe of Songshan Airport near the river. But I can taste the rain as it drips into my mouth and feel the cold wind as it unfurls against my limbs.

I long for a view, to see the island from a height, but it does not come. In this pale, damp firmament, there is no clearing. Instead, I have come to know the whiteness of a rain-cloaked canopy. I know the water that washes this place, spreading from the north; the sunlit fog that gathers at the heights of clouds; the trees that huddle green together, catching mist in their crowns.

I spend a few moments in that delicate cold, against the mantle of the island sky. Seeing only light, I make my way back down the mountain.

ACKNOWLEDGMENTS

Books make their way into the world with the support of many. A veritable 林—in Taiwan, Canada, the United Kingdom, the United States, Germany, Hong Kong, Australia—made this one possible.

To Megha Majumdar and Nicole Winstanley, thank you for understanding—sometimes implicitly— the story I set out to tell here. Your compassion as editors made this process all the better. To Lennie Goodings, thank you for your patience, guidance, and sharp-eyed edits as I brought this story out of the heady darkness.

David Godwin, my agent, who first heard me describe my grandparents' story at a traffic light on a busy street corner in Bloomsbury: thank you for loving the idea then and helping me advocate for it even when I couldn't see where I was going.

Lisette Verhagen and Philippa Sitters at DGA, you two make the process of writing and publishing so much brighter! Thank you for everything you do.

To the team at Catapult: Wah-Ming Chang and Heidi Ward, thank you for getting this manuscript into the best possible state. I'm so grateful for the time and attention you've put into this text. To the team at Virago in the U.K., especially Zoe Gullen, thank you for your meticulous edits.

Jasmine Gui, thank you for your detailed and thoughtful translation of my grandfather's letters. To my other translators, thank you for all that I cannot say here.

To all the people who helped me along the way in Taiwan: I cannot put in words the depth of hope and love I have for your country. Thank you. Any errors in this story are entirely my own.

Thanks to Josh and Celine for welcoming me into their Taipei home. Stu and Ross at Taiwan Adventures for leading me across Nenggao and delivering us all safely from the cliff's edge. Christoph for Kafka, city walks, and a flourishing of ideas. Julie for hiking insights, and Alejandro for enthusiasm on the trail. David for time, friendship, and making so much possible—also because you had a driver's license. Everyone at Dorm1828 for a quiet space. White

Wabbit Records for a soundtrack I played on repeat. Café LakuLaku (楽楽咖啡) in Taipei, Lorch und Söhne and Hermann Eicke in Berlin, thank you for endless days spent writing.

To Eddie Cheng 程鵬升 at the National Museum of Taiwan Literature, I am endlessly grateful. Thank you for guiding me through your exhibition, for all that you taught me about Taiwanese nature writing, and for the invitation to join "Taiwanese literature" with the publication of this book.

Charlene, the camerawoman who was my lens on the city and the decades my family missed: thank you for teaching me about the joys of coriander on ice cream, among so many other things. Anne for swims and belief. Kelsey and Simon for the spare bed and for being my constant cheerleaders and pretend parents. Joanna, for putting up with me for over twenty years (and for putting me up). Lifeguard Jane for constant support. Jessica, Chloe, Isla, and Tom for encouragement along the way. Steffi and Stefan for constant belief in my work, and their daughter Luca for her unfailing support of this book's title, so much so that she painted two trees onto a coffee mug long before the book was finished. Qian for patiently resuscitating my Mandarin over cups of chrysanthemum tea. Rachel and Alyssa, always, for everything, but especially for sending journal articles and reading drafts. Auntie Laura for nourishment and long-term perspective on my family. Jing-xien Ayi Popo for so much, but especially for welcoming us back into the fold.

A group of women—most of whom entered my life when I needed them most—gave me the strength and belief to write this book. To Emma-Lee, Doretta, Nine, Sennah, Joy, Ming, May-Lan, Traci, Rowan, and Doppelgänger Jess, my diasporic sisterhood: thank you for reminding me so often that this was a story to tell.

My family, thank you for your constant support. Thanks to my father for old photos, books, and ephemera from early visits to Taiwan. I kept them around me as I wrote.

Ricardo, thank you for so much, and especially for learning to say "turtle," "beer," "ice cream," and "I love you" in Mandarin. 我愛你!

Nika, the strongest (literally), most loving sister in the world. Thank you.

Momma, 沒有妳, 這個故事就不會存在. 謝謝妳. 我愛妳.

To my Gong and Po—Tsao Chung-chin 曹崇勤 and Yang Kwei-lin 楊桂琳—wherever you are now, I hope you know how loved you'll always be.

This work would not have been possible without

the generous support of an Authors' Foundation Grant from the Society of Authors and an Explore and Create grant from the Canada Council for the Arts. I'm thankful for the time they gave to me and this book, and for their support of so many authors hoping to get their stories on the page.

Last but not least: to those reading, thank you for taking the time to inhabit the island in these pages. I am ever grateful.

BIBLIOGRAPHY

LIBRARIES, ARCHIVES, AND DATABASES

Bayerische Staatsbibliothek: www.bsb-muenchen.de

British Library: www.bl.uk

Digital Taiwan: Culture and Nature, 2011: culture.teldap
.tw/culture/index.php

The International Plant Names Index (IPNI), 2012: www
.ipni.org

National Central Library of Taiwan: enwww.ncl.edu.tw

Plants of Taiwan Database of Historic Floras, 2014: tai2
.ntu.edu.tw

Staatsbibliothek zu Berlin: staatsbibliothek-berlin.de

Special Collections and Archives Division, History of
Aviation Archives, University of Texas at Dallas: www
.utdallas.edu/library/special-collections-and-archives

TEXTS

14th Air Force Association. *Chennault's Flying Tigers: 1941–1945*. Dallas: Taylor Publishing Company, 1982.

Adams, Frank Dawson. *The Birth and Development of the Geological Sciences*. Baltimore: The Williams and Wilkins Company, 1938.

Agnew, Duncan Carr. "History of Seismology." *International Handbook of Earthquake and Engineering Seismology* 81a (2002): 3–11.

Andrews, Susan. "Tree of the Year: Trochodendron aralioides." *International Dendrology Society Yearbook* (2009): 28–48.

Angiosperm Phylogeny Group. "An update of the Angiosperm Phylogeny Group classification for the orders and families of flowering plants: APG III." *The Botanical Journal of the Linnean Society* 161 (2009): 105–21.

Aspinwall, Nick. "Taiwan's Silent Forest Wars." *The Diplomat* (July 18, 2018). thediplomat.com/2018/07/taiwans-silent-forest-wars.

BirdLife International. "Machlolophus holsti." The IUCN Red List of Threatened Species 2016: e.T22711939A94313030 (2016).

———. "Platalea minor." The IUCN Red List of Threatened Species 2017: e.T22697568A119347801 (2017).

———. "Spotlight on flyways." BirdLife International Data Zone (2010). www.birdlife.org/datazone.

Birrell, Anne (trans.). *The Classic of Mountains and Seas*. London: Penguin, 1999.

Bourgon, Lyndsie. "How Forest Forensics Could Prevent the Theft of Ancient Trees." *Smithsonian Magazine* (September 6, 2017). www.smithsonianmag.com /science-nature/how-forest-forensics-could-prevent-the-theft-ancient-trees-180964731.

Central Geological Survey. "Geology of Taiwan." Central Geological Survey, MOEA (2018). twgeoref.moeacgs .gov.tw/GipOpenWeb/wSite/mp?mp=107.

Chang, Bi-yu. *Place, Identity, and National Imagination in Postwar Taiwan*. Abingdon: Routledge, 2015.

Chang, Kang-i Sun. *Journey Through the White Terror: A Daughter's Memoir*. Translated by Kang-i Sun Chang and Matthew Towns. Taipei: National Taiwan University Press, 2013.

Chang, Wen-Yen, Kuei-Pao Chen, and Yi- Ben Tsai. "An updated and refined catalog of earthquakes in Taiwan (1900–2014) with homogenized Mw magnitudes." *Earth, Planets and Space* 68, no. 45 (2016).

Ch'en, Kuo-tung. "Nonreclamation Deforestation in Taiwan, c. 1600–1976." In *Sediments of Time: Environment and Society in Chinese History*, edited by

Mark Elvin and Liu Ts'ui-jung, 693–727. Cambridge: Cambridge University Press, 1998.

Chen, Chi-Wen, Hitoshi Saito, and Takashi Oguchi. "Rainfall intensity–duration conditions for mass movements in Taiwan." *Progress in Earth and Planetary Science* (2015): 2–14.

Chen, C. Y., W. C. Lee, and F. C. Yu. "Debris flow hazards and emergency response in Taiwan." *Transactions on Ecology and the Environment* 90 (2006): 311–20.

Chen, Pingyuan. *Touches of History: An Entry into "May Fourth" China*. Translated by Michel Hockx, Maria af Sandeberg, Uganda Sze Pui Kwan, Christopher Neil Payne, and Christopher Rosenmeier. Leiden: Brill, 2011.

Chen, Tze-ying. "Protecting Ancient Beauty of Nature." *National Park Quarterly* (March 2009).

Chen, Wen-bin, and James Friesen. *An Illustrated Guide to Native Formosan Plants*. Taipei: Shulin Publishing Company, 2015. [Original Chinese-English Edition: 陳文彬, James Friesen. 看見台灣原生植物 (中英對照). 台北: 書林出版公司 發行人, 2015.]

Chen, Yi-Chang, Chen-Fa Wu, and Shin-Hwei Lin. "Mechanisms of Forest Restoration in Landslide Treatment Areas." *Sustainability* 6 (2014): 6766–80.

Chen, Zueng-Sang, Zeng-Yei Hseu, Chen-Chi Tsai. *The Soils of Taiwan*. Dordrecht: Springer, 2015.

Chennault, Claire Lee. *Way of a Fighter: The Memoirs of Claire Lee Chennault.* Edited by Robert Hotz. New York: G. P. Putnam's Sons, 1949.

Cheung, Dominic (trans.). *The Isle Full of Noises: Modern Chinese Poetry from Taiwan.* New York: Columbia University Press, 1987.

Cheung, Han. "Gas Bombing of the Sediq." *Taipei Times* (October 25, 2015).

Cheung, Raymond. *Aces of the Republic of China Air Force.* Oxford: Osprey, 2015.

Chiang, Tzen-Yuh, and Barbara A. Schaal. "Phylogeography of Plants in Taiwan and the Ryukyu Archipelago." *Taxon* 55 (2006): 31–41.

Chigira, Masahiro, Wen-Neng Wang, Takahiko Furuyac, and Toshitaka Kamai. "Geological causes and geomorphological precursors of the Tsaoling landslide triggered by the 1999 Chi-Chi earthquake, Taiwan." *Engineering Geology* 68 (2003): 259–73.

Chiu Yu-tzu. "In the shadow of giants." *Taipei Times* (September 30, 2002).

Chou, W. C., W. T. Lin, and C. Y. Lin. "Vegetation recovery patterns assessment at landslides caused by catastrophic earthquake: A case study in central Taiwan." *Environmental Monitoring and Assessment* (May 2009): 152–245.

Chou, Wan-yao. *A New Illustrated History of Taiwan.*

Translated by Carole Plackitt and Tim Casey. Taipei: SMC Publishing, 2015.

Chow, Tse-tsung. *The May Fourth Movement: Intellectual Revolution in Modern China*. Cambridge, MA: Harvard University Press, 1964.

Chung, Oscar. "Spoonbills, Wetlands, and Stories of Old Taiwan." *Taiwan Today* (April 1, 2010).

Council for Economic Planning and Development (ed.). *Adaptation Strategy to Climate Change in Taiwan*. Taipei: Council for Economic Planning and Development, 2012.

Craven, Wesley Frank, and James Lea Cate (eds.). *The Army Air Forces in World War II Volume IV: The Pacific—Guadalcanal to Saipan* (August 1942 to July 1944). Washington: Office of Air Force History, 1983.

Craven, Wesley Frank, and James Lea Cate (eds). *The Army Air Forces in World War II Volume VI: Men and Planes*. Washington: Office of Air Force History, 1983.

Croddy, Eric. "China's Role in the Chemical and Biological Disarmament Regimes." *The Nonproliferation Review* (Spring 2012): 16–47.

Crossley, John N. *Hernando de Los Ríos Coronel and the Spanish Philippines in the Golden Age*. Farnham: Ashgate, 2011.

Department of Forestry and Nature Conservation, Chinese Cultural University. "Long-term Ecological Study of Yangmingshan National Park: Vegetation changes and succession." Taipei: Office of the Ministry of the Interior: 2003. [Original in Chinese: 中國文化大學森林暨自然保育學系 研究主持人, 陽明山國家公園之長期生態研究: 植被變遷與演替調查. 內政部營建署陽明山國家公園管理處委託研究報告, 中華民國九十二年十二月.]

Donato, D. C., J. B. Kauffman, D. Murdiyarso, S. Kurnianto, M. Stidham, and M. Kanninen. "Mangroves among the most carbon-rich forests in the tropics." *Natural Geoscience* 4 (2011): 293–97.

Duke, N. C., J. O. Meyneke, S. Dittman, et al. "A world without mangroves?" *Science* 317 (2007): 41–42.

Elvin, Mark, and Liu Ts'ui-jung (eds). *Sediments of Time: Environment and Society in Chinese History.* Cambridge: Cambridge University Press, 1998.

Elwes, Henry John. *Memoirs of Travel, Sport, and Natural History.* Edited by Edward G. Hawke. London: Ernest Benn Limited, 1930.

Erwin, Kevin L. "Wetlands and Global Climate Change: The Role of Wetland Restoration in a Changing World." *Wetlands Ecology and Management* 17 (2009): 71–84.

Esherick, Joseph W. (ed). *Remaking the Chinese City: Modernity and National Identity, 1900–1950.* Honolulu: University of Hawai'i Press, 2000.

Fenby, Jonathan. *Generalissimo: Chiang Kai-shek and the China He Lost.* London: The Free Press, 2003.

——. *The Penguin History of Modern China: The Fall and Rise of a Great Power, 1850–2008.* London: Allen Lane, 2008.

Ferry, Timothy. "Wushe Legacy." *Taiwan Today* (November 1, 2010).

Frodin, David G. *A Guide to the Standard Floras of the World: An Annotated, Geographically Arranged Systematic Bibliography of the Principal Floras, Enumerations, Checklists and Chorological Atlases of Different Areas.* Cambridge: Cambridge University Press, 2010.

Gao, Pat. "Birding Taiwan." *Taiwan Today* (August 1, 2013).

Glosser, Susan L. *Chinese Visions of Family and State, 1915–1953.* Berkeley: University of California Press, 2003.

Grant, Rachel A., Tim Halliday, Werner P. Balderer, Fanny Leuenberger, Michelle Newcomer, Gary Cyr, and Friedemann T. Freund. "Ground Water Chemistry Changes before Major Earthquakes and Possible Effects on Animals." *International Journal of Environmental Research and Public Health* 8 (2011): 1936–56.

Greenwood, Sarah, Jan-Chang Chen, Chaur-Tzuhn Chen, and Alistair S. Jump. "Community change and species richness reductions in rapidly advancing tree lines." *Journal of Biogeography* (2016): 1–11.

Grimshaw, John. "Tree of the Year: Taiwania cryptomerioides." *International Dendrology Society Yearbook* (2010): 24–57.

Hayata, Bunzo. *Icones Plantarum Formosanarum.* Taihoku (Taipei): Bureau of Productive Industries, Government of Formosa, 1911–21.

He, Long-Yuan, Cindy Q. Tang, Zhao-Lu Wu, Huan-Chong Wang, Masahiko Ohsawa, and Kai Yan. "Forest structure and regeneration of the Tertiary relict Taiwania cryptomerioides in the Gaoligong Mountains, Yunnan, southwestern China." *Phytocoenologia* 45 (2015): 135–56.

Hsia, Li-Ming, and Ethan Yorgason. "Hou Shan in Maps: Orientalism in Taiwan's Geographic Imagination." *Taiwan in Comparative Perspective* 2 (2008): 1–20.

Hsiao, Mu-Chi. *A Field Guide to the Birds of Taiwan.* Taipei: Wild Bird Society of Taipei, 2018.

Hsiau, A-chin. *Contemporary Taiwanese Cultural Nationalism.* London: Routledge, 2000.

Huang, Cary. "Is Taiwan Trying to Erase Links to Mainland China, or Forget a Bloody Past?." *South China Morning Post* (December 16, 2017).

Huang, C-C., T-W. Hsu, H-V. Wang, Z-H. Liu, Y-Y. Chen, C-T. Chiu, et al. "Multilocus Analyses Reveal Postglacial Demographic Shrinkage of Juniperus morrisonicola (Cupressaceae), a Dominant Alpine Species in Taiwan." *PLoS ONE* 11.8 (2016): e0161713.

Huang, Tseng-chieng, et al. *Flora of Taiwan.* 2nd ed. Taipei: Editorial Committee of the Flora of Taiwan, 1994–2003.

Ikeya, Motoji. *Earthquakes and Animals: From Folk Legends to Science.* Singapore: World Scientific Publishing Co., 2004.

Jump, Alistair S., Tsung-Juhn Huang, and Chang-Hung Chou. "Rapid altitudinal migration of mountain plants in Taiwan and its implications for high altitude biodiversity." *Ecography* 35 (2012): 204–10.

Keating, Jerome F. *The Mapping of Taiwan: Desired Economies, Coveted Geographies.* Taipei: SMC Publishing, 2011.

Kim, Kwang-Hee, Chien-Hsin Chang, Kuo-Fong Ma, Jer-Ming Chiu, and Kou-Cheng Chen. "Modern Seismic Observations in the Tatun Volcano Region of Northern Taiwan: Seismic/Volcanic Hazard Adjacent to the Taipei Metropolitan Area." *TAO* 16.3 (2005): 579–94.

Leary, William. *The Dragon's Wings: The China National Aviation Corporation and the Development of*

Commercial Aviation in China. Athens: University of Georgia Press, 1976.

———. *Perilous Missions: Civil Air Transport and CIA Covert Operations in Asia*. Washington: Smithsonian Institution Press, 2002.

Lee, Shun-Ching. "Taiwan Red- and Yellow-Cypress and Their Conservation." *Taiwania* 8 (1962): 1–15.

Leeker, Joe F. *The History of Air America*. 2nd ed. Dallas: University of Texas Dallas, 2015. eBook. www.utdallas .edu/library/specialcollections/hac/cataam/Leeker /history.

Li, Hui-lin, et al. *Flora of Taiwan*. 1st ed. Taipei: Epoch Publishing Company, 1975–1979.

Li, Kuang-chün. "Mirrors and Masks: An Interpretive Study of Mainlanders' Identity Dilemma." *Memories of the Future: National Identity Issues and the Search for a New Taiwan*. Edited by Stéphane Corcuff. Armonk, NY: East Gate, 2002.

Liao, Chi-Cheng, Chang-Hung Chou, and Jiunn-Tzong Wu. "Regeneration patterns of yellow cypress on down logs in mixed coniferous-broadleaf forest of Yuanyang Lake Nature Preserve, Taiwan." *Botanical Bulletin of the Academia Sinica* 44 (2003): 229–38.

Liao, Ping-Hui, and David Der-Wei Wang (eds.). *Taiwan Under Japanese Colonial Rule, 1895–1945*. New York: Columbia University Press, 2006.

Lin, Chi-ko. "Alpine Plants in Taiwan Under the Influence of Climate Change." *National Park Quarterly* (December 2013).

Lin, Hsiao-ting. *Accidental State: Chiang Kai-shek, the United States, and the Making of Taiwan*. Cambridge, MA: Harvard University Press, 2016.

Lin, Sylvia Li-Chun. *Representing Atrocity in Taiwan: The 2/28 Incident and White Terror in Fiction and Film*. New York: Columbia University Press, 2007.

Liu, Kexiang. "Five Poems: 'Black Flight,' 'Island Song,' 'Guandu Life,' 'Black-Faced Spoonbill,' and 'Exile of the Mangroves.'" Translated by Nick Kaldis. *ISLE: Interdisciplinary Studies in Literature and Environment* 11, no. 2 (2004): 267–70.

Liu, Chia-Mei, Sheng-Rong Song, Yaw-Lin Chen, and Shuhjong Tsao. "Characteristics and Origins of Hot Springs in the Tatun Volcano Group in Northern Taiwan." *Terrestrial, Atmospheric and Oceanic Sciences* 22.5 (2011): 475–89.

Liu Ts'ui-jung. "Han Migration and the Settlement of Taiwan: The Onset of Environmental Change." In *Sediments of Time: Environment and Society in Chinese History*, eds. Mark Elvin and Liu Ts'ui-jung, 165–202. Cambridge: Cambridge University Press, 1998.

Lorge, Peter. *Chinese Martial Arts: From Antiquity to*

the Twenty-First Century. Cambridge: Cambridge University Press, 2012.

Lu, Shuping. *A Dark Page in History: The Nanjing Massacre and Post-massacre Social Conditions Recorded in British Diplomatic Dispatches, Admiralty Documents, and US Naval Intelligence Reports.* Lanham: University Press of America, 2012.

Luo, Bin, and Adam Grydehøj. "Sacred islands and island symbolism in Ancient and Imperial China: an exercise in decolonial island studies." *Island Studies Journal* 12, no. 12 (2017): 25–44.

Makeham, John, and A-chin Hsiau (eds). *Cultural, Ethnic, and Political Nationalism in Contemporary Taiwan.* New York: Palgrave Macmillan, 2005.

Mayo, Marlene J., J. Thomas Rimer, and H. Eleanor Kerkham (eds.). *War, Occupation, and Creativity: Japan and East Asia, 1920–1960.* Honolulu: University of Hawai'i Press, 2001.

Meigs, Doug. "The Black-faced Spoonbill: Asia's beloved wading bird fights for space." *Mongabay* (November 2, 2015): news.mongabay.com/2015/11/the-black-faced-spoonbill-asias-beloved-wading-bird-fights-for-space.

Ministry of National Defence, ROC. *The Immortal Flying Tigers: An Oral History of the Chinese-American Composite Wing.* Taipei: Military History and Translation Office, Ministry of National Defense, 2009.

Mitra, O., et al. "Grunting for Worms: Seismic Vibrations Cause Diplocardia Earthworms to Emerge from the Soil." *Biology Letters* 5.1 (2009): 16–19.

Musson, R. M. W. "A History of British Seismology." *Bulletin of Earthquake Engineering* 11 (2013): 715–861.

National Taiwan Museum of Fine Art. "The 'Regional Flavor' of Art in Taiwan During the Japanese Colonial Era." *The Development of Taiwanese Art: Digital Exhibition Catalogue* (2007): taiwaneseart.ntmofa.gov.tw/english/Eb3_1.html.

Ohashi, Hiroyoshi. "Bunzo Hayata and His Contributions to the Flora of Taiwan." *Taiwania* 54.1 (2009): 1–27.

Pan, Jason. "Tree DNA database aims to combat illegal logging." *Taipei Times* (June 29, 2017).

Pocock, Chris, and Clarence Fu. *The Black Bats: CIA Spy Flights over China from Taiwan, 1951–1969.* Atglen: Schiffer Military History, 2010.

Ross, Pauline M., and Paul Adam. "Climate Change and Intertidal Wetlands." *Biology* (Basel) vol. 2, issue 1 (2013): 445–80.

Roy, Denny. *Taiwan: A Political History.* Ithaca: Cornell University Press, 2003.

Rubinstein, Murray A. *Taiwan: A New History.* Armonk, NY: M. E. Sharpe, 1999.

Shen, Eugene Yu-Feng. "Plants of Unusual Economic Value on Taiwan." *Taiwania* 7 (1960): 105–11.

Shen, Grace Yen. *Unearthing the Nation: Modern Geology and Nationalism in Republican China.* Chicago: University of Chicago Press, 2014.

Shen, Kuo. *Brush Talks from Dream Brook.* Translated by Wang Hong and Zhao Zheng. Chengdu: Sichuan People's Publishing House/Paths International, 2011.

Shimoda, Brandon. "The Papaya Tree." *Evening Will Come* 67 (2017).

Sibueta, Jean-Claude, and Shu-Kun Hsu. "How was Taiwan Created?." *Tectonophysics* 379 (2004): 159–81.

Simon, Scott. "Taiwan's Mainlanders: A Diasporic Identity in Construction." *Revue européenne des migrations internationales,* vol. 22, no. 1 (2009): 1–18.

Sui, Cindy. "Why bamboo is booming again in Taiwan." *BBC News* (9 April 2014).

Stafleu, Frans A., and Richard S. Cowan. *Taxonomic literature: A selective guide to botanical publications and collections with dates, commentaries and types.* Utrecht: Bohn, Scheltema and Holkema, 1976–88.

Swennen, Cornelis, and Yat-Tung Yu. "Food and Feeding Behaviour of the Black-Faced Spoonbill." *Waterbirds: The International Journal of Waterbird Biology* 28, no. 1 (March 2005): 19–27.

Swinhoe, Robert. "Notes on the Island of Formosa." *Journal of the Royal Geographical Society of London* 34 (1864): 6–18.

Takegami, Mariko. "The Origins of Modern Geology in China: The Work of D. J. Macgowan and R. Pumpelly," *Zinbun* 46 (2015): 179–97.

Teng, Emma Jinhua. *Taiwan's Imagined Geography: Chinese Colonial Travel Writing and Pictures, 1683–1895*. Cambridge, MA: Harvard University Press, 2004.

Thomson, J. "Notice of a Journey in Southern Formosa." *Proceedings of the Royal Geographical Society of London* 17, no. 3 (1872–1873): 144–48.

Thornber, Karen Laura. *Ecoambiguity: Environmental Crises and East Asian Literatures*. Ann Arbor: University of Michigan Press, 2012.

Tsai, Tehpen. *Elegy of Sweet Potatoes: Stories of Taiwan's White Terror*. Translated by Grace Hatch. Upland, California: Taiwan Publishing Co., 2002.

Tsou, Chih-Hua, and Scott A. Mori. "Seed Coat Anatomy and its relationship to seed dispersal in subfamily Lecythidoidieae of the Lecythidaceae (The Brazil Nut Family)." *Botanical Bulletin of Academia Sinica* 43 (2002): 37–56.

Tung, An-Chi. "Hydroelectricity and Industrialization: The Economic, Social, and Environmental Impacts of the Sun Moon Lake Power Plants." In *Sediments of Time: Environment and Society in Chinese History*, eds. Mark Elvin and Liu Ts'ui-jung, 728–55. Cambridge: Cambridge University Press, 1998.

Vava, Hulusman, Auvini Kadresengan, Badai, Shu-hwa Shirley Wu, and John M. Anderson. *Voices from the Mountain: Taiwanese Aboriginal Literature: English Translation Series.* Taiwan: Serenity International, 2014.

Williams, Jack, and Ch'ang-yi David Chang. *Taiwan's Environmental Struggle: Towards a Green Silicon Island.* London: Routledge, 2008.

Wright, David. "The Translation of Modern Western Science in Nineteenth-Century China, 1840–1895," *Isis* 89.4 (1998): 653–73.

Wu Ming-Yi. *The Man with the Compound Eyes.* Translated by Darryl Sterk. London: Vintage, 2014.

———. *The Stolen Bicycle.* Translated by Darryl Sterk. Melbourne: Text Publishing, 2017.

Xia, Mingfang. "The Ecology of Home." *RCC Perspectives: Transformations in Environment and Society.* Munich: Rachel Carson Centre, 2017.

Yang, Bao-yu. "Studies on Taiwan Mosses: Notes on Three Noteworthy Mosses of Taiwan." *Taiwania* 8 (1962): 29–33.

Yang, Dominic Meng-Hsuan, and Mau-Kuei Chang. "Understanding the Nuances of *Waishengren*." *China Perspectives* (2010): 108–22.

Yang, Linhui, and Denming An, with Jessica Anderson Turner. *Handbook of Chinese Mythology.* Santa Barbara: ABC-Clio, 2005.

Yangmingshan National Park. "The Topology of the Datun Volcano Group" (November 29, 2011): www.ymsnp.gov.tw/main_en/.

Yeh, Benjamin. "Rising Sea Levels Threaten Taiwan." *Taipei Times* (May 10, 2010).

Yen, Chuan-ying. "Colonial Taiwan and the Construction of Landscape Painting." In *Taiwan Under Japanese Colonial Rule, 1895–1945*, eds. Liao, Ping-Hui, and David Der-Wei Wang, 248–61. New York: Columbia University Press, 2006.

Yen, T. M. "Relationships of Chamaecyparis formosensis crown shape and parameters with thinning intensity and age." *Annals of Forest Research* 58.2 (2015): 323–32.

Yu, Yonghe. *Small Sea Travel Diaries: Yu Yonghe's Records of Taiwan*. Translated by Macabe Keliher. Taipei: SMC Publishing, 2004.

© Ricardo Rivas

JESSICA J. LEE is a British Canadian Taiwanese author and environmental historian, and winner of the 2019 RBC Taylor Prize Emerging Writer Award. She received a doctorate in environmental history and aesthetics in 2016, and her first book, *Turning: A Year in the Water*, was published in 2017. Lee is the founding editor of *The Willowherb Review*. She lives in Berlin. Find out more at www.jessicajleewrites.com.

🐦 @jessicajlee

📷 @jessicajlee